Johannes Brahms

1833-1897

Gustav Mahler

1869-1911

Staff Credits

Editors
David Buxton BA (Honours)
Sue Lyon BA (Honours)

Art Editors
Debbie Jecock BA (Honours)
Ray Leaning BA (Honours), PGCE (Art & Design)

Deputy Editor
Barbara Segall BA

Sub-editors
Geraldine Jones
Judy Oliver BA (Honours)
Nigel Rodgers BA (Honours), MA
Penny Smith
Will Steeds BA (Honours), MA

Designers
Steve Chilcott BA (Honours)
Shirin Patel BA (Honours)
Chris Rathbone

Picture Researchers
Georgina Barker
Julia Calloway BA (Honours)
Vanessa Cawley

Production Controllers
Sue Fuller
Steve Roberts

Secretary
Lynn Smail

Publisher
Terry Waters Grad IOP

Editorial Director
Maggi McCormick

Production Executive
Robert Paulley BSc

Managing Editor
Alan Ross BA (Honours)

Consultants
Dr Antony Hopkins
Commander of the Order of the British Empire, Fellow of the Royal College of Music

Nick Mapstone BA (Honours), MA

Keith Shadwick BA (Honours)

Reference Edition Published 1990
Published by Marshall Cavendish Corporation
147 West Merrick Road
Freeport, Long Island
N.Y. 11520

Typeset by Walkergate Press Ltd, Hull, England
Printed and bound in Singapore by
Times Offset Private Ltd.

Library of Congress Cataloging-in-Publication Data

The Great composers, their lives and times.

Includes index.
1. Composers—Biography. 2. Music appreciation.
I. Marshall Cavendish Corporation.
ML390.G82 1987 780' 92'2 [B] 86-31294
ISBN 0-86307-776-5

ISBN 0-86307-776-5 (set)
0-86307-783-8 (vol)

Johannes Brahms

1833-1897

Gustav Mahler

1869-1911

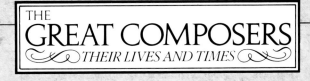

MARSHALL CAVENDISH
NEW YORK · LONDON · SYDNEY

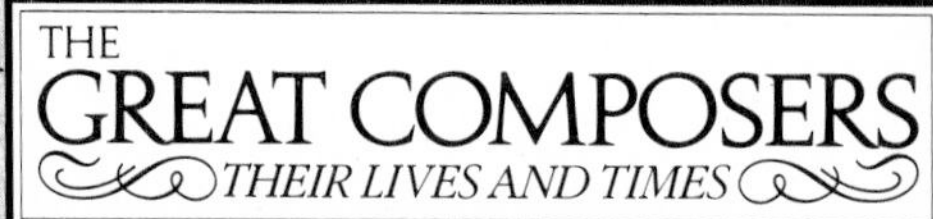
THE
GREAT COMPOSERS
THEIR LIVES AND TIMES

Contents

Introduction

As the 19th century entered its second half, the musical idioms epitomized by Beethoven and his followers were under attack. Romantic composers like Liszt revered the great masters of the past and respected their achievements, but believed that musical form should change and develop. Those opposed to the 'New Music' looked to Johannes Brahms as their champion. Brahms was indeed the last great composer of the Classical tradition, and like his predecessors Mozart and Beethoven, was able to compose in all musical forms, including the symphony, choral works and short piano pieces.

In 1890, the elderly Brahms was persuaded to see Gustav Mahler conduct a performance of Don Giovanni *in Budapest. Brahms was very impressed and, though he never liked Mahler's compositions, did much to help his later career. As a conductor, Mahler won early recognition; his reputation as a composer took longer to establish. Like Brahms, Mahler was the last great composer of an old tradition – that of Vienna – and in his work can be seen both the culmination of that tradition and the beginnings of the 20th-century idiom. He drew together the strands of Romanticism: Beethoven's symphonic form; the programme music of Liszt and Tchaikovsky; Wagner's expanded orchestra and emotional intensity; and Schubert and Bruckner's folk style. In his later works major motifs of modern music – lack of tonality, chamber orchestration, and tonal dissonance – are present, and Mahler has exerted great influence over composers like Schoenberg, Webern, Shostakovich, Britten and other giants of 20th-century music.*

THE GREAT COMPOSERS

Johannes Brahms

1833-1897

Contemporaries saw Johannes Brahms as the successor to Beethoven to such an extent that his first symphony was nicknamed 'Beethoven's Tenth'. Like his great predecessor, Brahms came from a poor and humble background, but unlike Beethoven his home life was happy and, as Composer's Life *describes, his family encouraged the young Johannes's musical talents. Brahms was also helped by Robert Schumann, the composer and powerful music critic. As can be heard in Brahms's music – some of his greatest works are analyzed in the* Listener's Guide *– he was greatly influenced by Schumann, and as a result was cast as one of the leading figures in the battle against the new music of Liszt and Wagner.* In the Background *describes how times were changing outside music: economic hardship led many Germans to emigrate; Germany was being transformed by Bismark into a powerful empire; and the railway revolution for the first time enabled ordinary people to travel widely.*

COMPOSER'S LIFE

'Pure as a diamond'

Cautious and shy by nature, Brahms found it difficult to show his true feelings. It was only through his music that he was able to express his warmth of heart and utter sincerity.

Brahms was born in Hamburg on 7 May, 1833. His ather, Johann Jakob Brahms, was an orchestral double bass player who married a woman 17 years older than iimself. But Christiane, although 41 when they narried, soon gave him three children of whom the composer, Johannes Brahms, was the second.

The Brahms household seems to have been happy ınd respectable, though poor. Johannes was sent to a orivate school and later to a grammar school. Outside his academic studies his two passions seem to have been his collection of toy soldiers (which he kept into adulthood) and – of course – music. In 1840 he began piano lessons with a teacher called Friedrich Wilhelm Cossel, and within three years Cossel had unselfishly passed him on to his own distinguished teacher Eduard Marxsen. Marxsen seems to have known from the first that he was dealing with genius, or something very like it, and although his first aim was to turn his pupil into a brilliant pianist he soon recognized that an exceptional creative gift also had to be encouraged and guided.

His piano-playing skill did, however, lead the young Brahms into some experiences that were to leave a kind of scar on his adult life. From around the age of 13 he used to play, for food and minimal payment, in the dockland bars near his home which were effectively sailors' brothels. The atmosphere into which this highly sensitive teenager was inevitably drawn seems to have been sordid in the extreme; sometimes he tried to block it out by putting a book of poems on the

A tender portrait of Brahms (above) at the age of 20 (1853). In his youth he had a rather delicate face framed by long flaxen hair. As one lady-friend put it: 'He had the face of a child, which any girl could kiss without a blush.' It was perhaps to hide his rather effeminate looks that Brahms later grew the distinctive white beard which gave him his familiar, avuncular image.

Courtesy of Victoria and Albert Museum

Archiv für Kunst und Geschichte, Berlin

The young Brahms came into contact with Hungarian folk music (above), following the influx into Hamburg of refugees after the 1848 Hungarian uprising.

The house where Brahms was born (right) – a cramped tenement building in the poor area of old Hamburg.

music stand in front of him and simply playing popular tunes mechanically. He never forgot experience, and sometimes talked about it bitterly later life.

A career begins

At the age of 17, Brahms was already on the thresh of a successful musical career. He got to know Hungarian-Jewish violinist called Eduard Remér Reményi was three years older than Johannes colourful character who specialized in play brilliant gypsy-style music as well as the stand classics; he was also a bit of a revolutionary who extensive travels had at least partly been caused by need to evade the police.

He and Brahms set off on a joint concert tour ea in 1853 and during the trip Reményi introduced companion to another and more distinguish violinist, Joseph Joachim, who served the King Hanover as principal violinist. Joachim was impress by Brahms's playing and even more so by his pia compositions, which at this time included son movements and a powerful Scherzo in E flat min This, he later declared, was music of 'undreamt originality and power'. Joachim arranged for the tv travellers to play to the King, offered Brahms (but n it seems, Reményi) a special open invitation to retu at any time, and provided a letter of introduction the great pianist-composer Franz Liszt.

At the Court of Weimar, whose music he directe Liszt received Reményi and Brahms graciously. T shy to play himself, Johannes was both astonished a admiring when Liszt took his Scherzo manuscript a

Museen der Stadt Wien/Bridgeman Art Library.

Brahms c.1860 (left) – an intensely romantic young man. If he had not been so short, Brahms would have been a very imposing figure, with his high brow, penetrating blue eyes and finely-chiselled features.

Throughout his life, Brahms had a deep love of the countryside, delighting in the natural beauty of the Swiss and Austrian scenery (right). For him, it was not only a welcome refuge from the pressures of city living, but also a lasting inspiration for many of his compositions.

ght-read it with great aplomb, meanwhile offering a mplimentary running commentary. In turn, Liszt d his listeners the very considerable compliment of aying for them his own recently completed Piano nata in B minor – all the more of a privilege in that is greatest among living pianists no longer gave iblic recitals. Brahms must surely have been ipressed. But perhaps because of his natural shyness, was less than extravagantly fulsome in his praise. hether Liszt felt offended we may only guess. But ményi, the more practised courtier (and probably e shallower musician) was angry, feeling that his oung partner had alienated a celebrated musician hose goodwill was of much professional value to m. He told Brahms that their association must end.

Brahms had no money. Was he to return dejectedly Hamburg, where his father had already plainly dicated his wish to see his gifted son successfully anding on his own feet? Instead he wrote to Joachim: can't return to Hamburg without anything to show . . .' ight he, please, visit Joachim, who was to spend the immer at the university town of Göttingen attending me of the lectures? An immediate 'yes' brought the o young musicians together again, and a long-lasting endship and musical understanding developed.

e Schumanns

or some time Brahms had respected the reputation of e composer Robert Schumann, without knowing a eat deal of his music. During 1853, however, both achim and other musical friends had brought him a ider knowledge of Schumann's work and Joachim ged him to visit Schumann at his home in Düsseldorf. Finally Brahms overcame his hesitation and made up his mind. On 30 September, 1853 he knocked on Schumann's door, was welcomed and at once taken to the piano to play his C major Sonata. But he had not gone far when Schumann stopped him. 'Clara must hear this', he cried and went from the room to fetch his pianist wife. We have Clara Schumann's own diary account of what happened after this:

He played us sonatas, scherzos etc. of his own, all showing exuberant imagination, depth of feeling and mastery of form. Robert says there was nothing he could tell him to take away or add. It is really moving to see him sitting at the piano, with his interesting young face, which becomes transfigured when he plays, his beautiful hands, which overcome the greatest difficulties . . . what he played to us is so masterly that one can only think the good God sent him ready-made into the world. He has a great future before him, for he will find the first true field for his genius when he begins to write for orchestra.

Robert Schumann's reaction to his young visitor was like that of his wife, immediate and wholehearted. A diary entry for the day of their first meeting reads simply, 'Brahms to see me – a genius'. Johannes was virtually taken into the Schumann household and throughout October 1853 enjoyed an artistic environment of a richness such as he had never known before. As for Schumann, he was determined that Brahms's name, and his music too, should at once become more widely known.

Brahms (seated) with the distinguished violinist, Joseph Joachim (below). The two became firm friends and developed a sympathetic and fruitful musical partnership.

Courtesy of the Map House, London

Bildarchiv Preussischer Kulturbesitz

Tragedies and passions

Schumann's support and friendship were a magnificent stimulus, and Brahms rejoiced with them. But his close involvement with the older composer and his family was to draw him into a tragic situation. Schumann was a manic-depressive with a long history of mental illness, generally believed to have been due to syphilis. He had for some time been alarming Clara by long brooding silences and even hallucinations. Then on 27 February, 1854 he left his house and threw himself into the River Rhine. He was dragged out by a boat crew, but remained in a state of mental confusion. Within a few days he had been declared insane and was removed to an institution where he was to remain until his death two years later.

As soon as he heard the news, Brahms rushed to Clara's side. Prostrated by her husband's tragedy, and halfway through a pregnancy, she came to depend heavily on the support of her devoted young friend. Since she was not allowed to visit Schumann for fear of over-exciting him, Brahms acted as an occasional go-between, visiting her husband, who had some lucid periods. It must have put an immense strain on a deeply sensitive young man, particularly as he had fallen in love with Clara.

In the meantime Clara Schumann, with seven children to feed, had to work to earn a living. She, together with Brahms and Joachim, gave a series of concerts, and she made a point of playing Brahms's music. He, too, gave piano recitals in Bremen, Leipzig and his native Hamburg. But on the whole he was not a tremendous success: it seems that the 'flavour' of his big sonatas, sternly romantic as they were, was not to everyone's taste. His residence was now in Düsseldorf, near Clara, and he may have hoped to be offered the municipal directorship of music formerly held by Schumann. But that hope came to nothing. In the meantime, however, he remained in Düsseldorf, where it was soon clear that he was doing little to advance his career as a composer. His parents, and his old teacher Marxsen, became worried.

Some, if not all, of the reason for Brahms's residence in Düsseldorf must have been his growing love for Clara Schumann. She was ten years younger than her dying husband and still an attractive woman only approaching her mid-30s. 'I wish I could tell you how deeply I love you', he wrote to her in a letter. No one knows whether their relationship ever took a physical form, but most people think it unlikely. Clara took her role as a soon-to-be-widowed young mother very seriously. She became friendly with Brahms's mother, assuring her that she would stand by Johannes 'always, with true affection'. In theory, the idea of marriage to Clara may have attracted him. But when Schumann died and this became actually possible, he decided instead to leave Düsseldorf. He remained a devoted friend to Clara and her children, but there was to be no more talk of love between them.

Detmold and Vienna

From 1857 to 1860 Brahms held a court appointment as Director of Music to the princely court of Detmold, 60 miles south-west of Hanover. He taught the princess the piano and conducted a choir; as well as this he played the piano at concerts and had a number of private pupils whose fees augmented his salary. There was a court orchestra for which he composed two serenades. At this time also he completed his very un-courtly First Piano Concerto (1858), a stormy work which had occupied him since Schumann's illness and which almost certainly reflected his

Archiv für Kunst und Geschichte, Berlin

abms first visited enna (right) in the ring of 1863 and mediately felt the arm of the Austrian pital. He wrote to a end: 'The gaiety of the vn, the beauty of the rroundings, the npathetic and acious public: how mulating these are to e artist! In addition we ve in particular the emory of the great usicians whose lives d works are brought ily to our minds.' ter, in the early 1870s, was to make the city of ethoven and Schubert s permanent home.

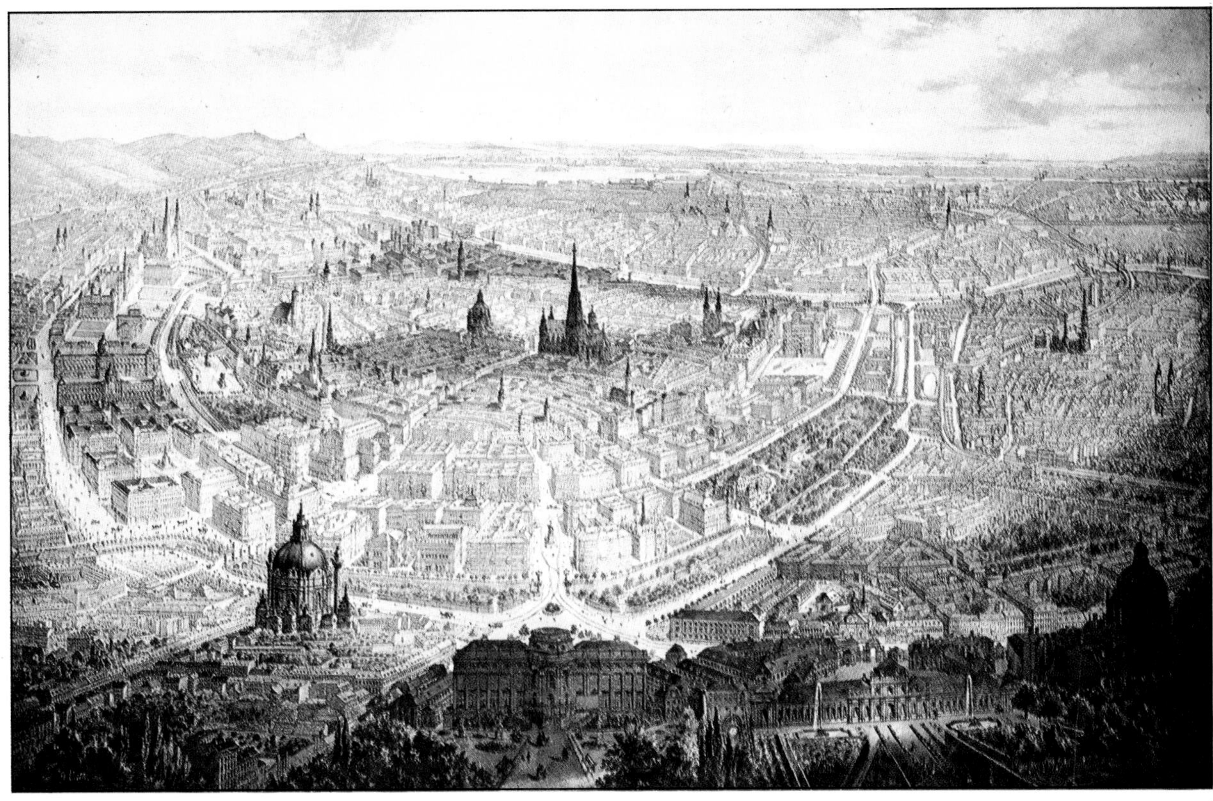

Archiv für Kunst und Geschichte, Berlin

***abms's own musical stes were wide-nging and refreshingly e from intellectual obbery. He loved the usic of Vienna's waltz-ng, Johann Strauss – ayed here by an all-nale orchestra (left) – st as much as he had ved the Hungarian psy music in Hamburg. once admitted that would have given ything to have written e* Blue Danube.**

abms quickly settled wn to the lively social e in Vienna (below), joying the food and ink as much as the mpany.

turbulent feelings at that time. It had its first performance in Hanover on 22 January, 1859, with Joachim as conductor and the composer himself as soloist; and Brahms played it again a few days later in Leipzig. But the audience reaction was cool, even hostile. Brahms wrote to Joachim: 'It will please one day . . . after all I'm still trying . . . all the same, the hissing was a bit much.'

Detmold and court duties were agreeable and well paid, but they occupied Brahms for only a few months of each year. He still spent part of his time with his family in Hamburg, but now acquired a house of his own in an attractive suburb. In Hamburg he founded a women's choir, which he conducted and trained; he composed music for them as well. Perhaps it was inevitable that this young man, still in his mid-20s, should have been attracted to one of his singers, called Bertha Porubsky. She was actually a visitor from Vienna, and Brahms liked to hear her sing her native Austrian folk songs. The romance, if such it was, ended when she returned to Vienna and married. But she and her husband remained friendly with Brahms, and it was for her first-born child that the composer later wrote what must be his most famous song, the *Cradle Song*, a tender and lilting lullaby.

Archiv für Kunst und Geschichte, Berlin

Another woman in his life was also a singer. Agathe von Siebold was the daughter of a university professor at Göttingen, where Brahms had gone to stay with friends. She seems to have loved him, and he her: they enjoyed music-making together, and going for long hill walks. His friends were all certain that their engagement would soon be announced. But it never happened. 'I love you', he wrote to Agathe: 'I must see you again. But I *can't* wear chains. Write and tell me if I can return to take you in my arms'. She was deeply hurt, and Brahms too had the grace to feel guilty about his apparently callous behaviour. After that he was more cautious in his relationships with women. In fact, of his sex life nothing whatever is known for certain – even if he had one at all. Some of his biographers suggest he may have patronized prostitutes, associating sex indissolubly with the Hamburg of his childhood, but remaining unable to enter into more serious attachments. Certainly he never again got close to marriage, and found himself forced to make a joke of it: namely that when he wanted to marry he could not afford it but when he finally had enough money no girl would have him. A remark by Nietzsche to the effect that Brahms's music betrayed 'the melancholy of impotence' may have hinted unkindly at something more. For as a young man Brahms had a high-pitched voice and almost feminine prettiness, as well as small stature; it may have been to disguise this that he later grew a large beard.

Meanwhile, as he approached 30, his music was becoming better known. Clara Schumann played the piano works, Joachim played the violin in his chamber music and conducted orchestral pieces, and a singer called Julius Stockhausen took the Brahms songs into his repertoire, sometimes with the composer himself playing the piano. The particular style of his music, too, was beginning to be appreciated and to take its place in the scheme of things. But the critical response was distorted by the musical infighting of the time and his music only gained recognition slowly.

From 1862 Brahms made his home in Vienna. There he conducted a choir and enjoyed the pleasures of a city that still remembered Beethoven and Schubert. He met Wagner too and was not too proud to help copy out orchestral parts of *Die Meistersinger* for a Viennese performance of part of that opera. Leading players of chamber music seized on Brahms's music, and one called him 'Beethoven's heir'. He played his own *Handel Variations* for piano with success, a the Viennese also heard his orchestral serenad Somehow, what with the various strands of his musi activity, he managed to make quite a comfortal living. When his parents separated, he helped mother to set up in a small flat of her own in Hambu and he was heart-broken, from all accounts, when s died in 1865. Her death at least partly inspired him complete the *German Requiem,* first heard thr years later. It was the *German Requiem* that ma Brahms's name and established him financially.

The routine of Brahms's life, centring on Viennese home, was gradually established. T autumn and spring often found him on concert tou as a pianist and conductor. In the winter he was mus making and composing in Vienna, and in the summ he liked to holiday at Lichtenthal, where Cl Schumann kept a cottage and where the old frien could meet and exchange memories and news.

Brahms happily poses with two daughters of a friend (below), during a summer visit to Gmunden.

Österreichische Nationalbibliothek

The last decades

It was in 1876 that Brahms finally completed his Fi Symphony. The idea for such a work had haunted hi since the time of his first encounter with t Schumanns long before, and he had shown Clara sor sketches in 1862. He found the big horn solo of t symphony's finale in a 'shepherd's horn' idea in 18 which he passed on to Clara complete with 'alpir words perhaps of his own invention. The symphon première in 1876 came after a four-year 'orchestr period following his appointment in 1872 as direct of the Vienna Philharmonic Society, which had al seen the successful performance of his *Requiem* and Anthony' Variations under his direction as well much other old and new music. This golden period Brahms's 40s and early 50s saw the creation of some his most important orchestral works: three mo

The mezzo-soprano Hermine Spies (below), who we Brahms's close friend during his middle age (his dear 'Herminchen'). Her considerable talent and fun-loving nature inspired a rich outpouring of ne songs from the composer.

In 1853, Brahms called on the celebrated composer Robert Schumann (far left). Schumann's reaction to the young Brahms was immediate and whole-hearted. He hailed the young composer as a 'genius', and became his staunch friend and most vociferous champion.

No less enthusiastic was Schumann's wife, Clara (left), a famous pianist in her own right. Brahms developed a desperate love for Clara – 14 years his senior – and was by her side throughout her husband's tragic illness and death in 1856. Later, this youthful infatuation matured into a devoted friendship.

An imposing portrait of Brahms (below) at the age of 58.

Bildarchiv Preussischer Kulturbesitz

·mphonies (the Fourth, his last, dates from 1885), as ·ell as the Violin Concerto and the Second Piano oncerto. There was also the *Academic Festival ·verture* written in 1880 for the University of Breslau ·hich gave the composer an honorary degree. This ·as a time of both artistic and material success: ·gether with his publisher of the Viennese years, ·imrock, Brahms now earned a considerable income ·om his music. He also had influence and was able to ·elp a gifted young composer, Dvořák, by helping him) find a publisher just as Schumann had done for him ·ears before.

But he continued to live fairly simply, in relatively ıodest lodgings. He kept up with his old friends, like ·lara Schumann, and with newer ones like the ·mateur pianist Elisabeth von Herzogenberg whom he ·ot to know well in 1874 and to whom he wrote ·scinating and artistically revealing letters. With ·ther friends, relations were sometimes less easy. He ·ffended the pianist and conductor Hans von Bülow, ·ne of his strongest supporters, by conducting his ·ourth Symphony in Frankfurt just before Bülow and ·is own orchestra were to perform it in the same city. ·here was trouble, too, with one of his oldest and most ·yal friends, Joachim, when Brahms took his wife's ·ide in a marital upset. Brahms had written to ·achim's wife expressing his belief in her innocence ·llowing her jealous husband's accusation of ·dultery; when the case came to the divorce court, ·achim's suit was defeated partly on the evidence of ·rahms's letter which was read aloud. Shattered, ·achim denounced his 'disloyal friend' and broke off ·elations with him. Later they patched matters up, not ·ast with the Double Concerto for Violin and Cello 1887) in which Joachim played the violin at the ·remière.

The concerto was Brahms's last orchestral work. He ·ad entered into an autumnal period. Although only in ·is 50s, he found things changing about him. He put on ·eight and travelled less far and less frequently. He ·rote fine shorter pieces for piano and his Clarinet ·uintet, but the *Four Serious Songs* (1896), with their

Bildarchiv Preussischer Kulturbesitz

Bildarchiv Preussischer Kulturbesitz

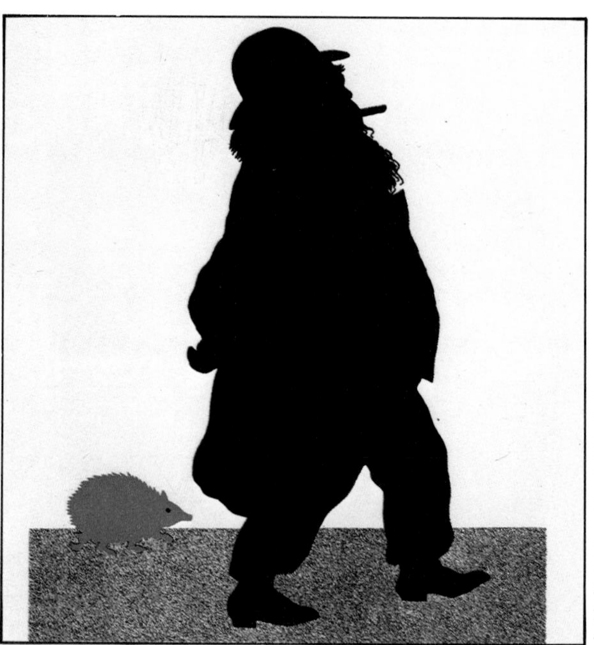

Archiv für Kunst und Geschichte, Berlin

A familiar sight in Vienna: Brahms striding purposefully towards his favourite eating place at dusk, hands behind his back (above). In this typical pose, he has been captured by a caricaturist (above right) – who seems to have been familiar with Brahms's eating habits. The hedgehog alludes to the 'Red Hedgehog' restaurant, while also hinting at Brahms's prickly nature.

Biblical texts, must be songs of farewell. His sister Elise and his friend Elisabeth von Herzogenberg both died in 1892, von Bülow in 1894, and Clara Schumann in 1896. He heard this last news while on holiday and rushed to be at Clara's funeral at Frankfurt. He arrived too late for the service and had to travel on to Bonn, where Clara was to be laid beside her husband. The 36 hours of lonely, brooding travel took their toll, however: Clara had meant more to him than any woman save perhaps his mother, and her loss was perhaps even more of a shock than he had expected. The *Four Serious Songs* which he had composed only weeks before had been concerned with mortality: indeed, the third of them begins with the words 'O Death, how bitter art thou!'. Now it was time to think, and without delay, about his own end.

Re-established in Vienna, Brahms sought coura geously to pick up the threads of his working an social life. But he was clearly unwell: his face began t take on a yellow tinge and friends became anxious Finally he saw a doctor, apparently asking, with hollow humour, not to be told 'anything unpleasant Jaundice was diagnosed, and he was sent to a spa town Karlsbad, to 'take the waters'. But the doctors told hi friends a different story. Brahms was seriously ill. Lik his father before him, who had died in 1872, Brahm had cancer. He was never told, but it was clear that h knew himself to be doomed. He lost weight alarmingly and became very tired. Finally, lovingly watched ove by his landlady and friend, Frau Truxa, he died in hi bed on 3 April, 1897.

Personality and achievement

Like Beethoven, Brahms was short, less than five fee six inches in height. He was fair, with bright an penetrating blue eyes and a high-pitched voice whicl in later life he disguised by gruffness. He grew hi distinctive beard in 1878, became grey soon after 50 and finally grew fat (until his last, wasting illness). H enjoyed his food, but was not extravagant or exotic ir his gastronomic tastes, and his clothes, though clean were somewhat untidy and unfashionable. I company he could be offhand and even rude, though i seems to have been uncouthness rather than malic that led to such incidents: like Beethoven, who coul also offend, the character of the man (and of course hi genius) ensured that his friends uncomplainingly endured temporary slights of which Brahms himsel was often unaware. With children, and animals too, h was more at ease: they liked him and he them Children often followed him about while he was o holiday, and he encouraged them to do so. Once when a girl gave him a rose, he asked, 'Is that sup posed to represent my prickly nature?' She had n idea what he meant; but she, and many others like her

Brahms celebrating the wedding anniversary of his friends the Fellingers in the summer of 1896 (right).

One of Brahms's greatest pleasures was travel. He visited Italy no less than eight times between 1878 and 1893. His enthusiasm for the country was immense. As a friend related: 'Brahms bubbles with desire to speak Italian, has studied grammar for months and learnt all the irregular verbs.'

:new that Herr Brahms was essentially a kindly man who made a careful choice of toys or sweets for presents, and above all had patience with his younger riends.

Quite early in life, Brahms seems to have lost any orthodox Christian faith. Yet the composer of the *German Requiem* and the *Four Serious Songs,* or for that matter the Alto Rhapsody of 1869 with its deeply serious text by Goethe, was clearly very conscious of he eternal questions of life and death. He faced his own death with something like stoicism, though his unwillingness to hear the harsh truth from his doctors, preferring a fiction which could be kept up until the very last, is rather touching. His evident human vulnerability, and tenderness too, always lay beneath a cautious, sometimes even suspicious surface personality: but where Brahms gave his affection and trust it was given wholeheartedly and (as far as he was concerned) for life.

Whether or not we understand Joachim's description of his friend as 'pure as a diamond, soft as snow', we may agree with what that perhaps implies, a quality which stands out in all Brahms's music and which may make it especially valuable in today's uncertain world – namely its utter sincerity. Brahms may have found it hard to express individual human love in a relationship such as marriage; but his warmth of heart found expression in his music, informing every piece he wrote, particularly the mellow later works. For that we shall always be grateful.

A fond picture of Brahms, taken towards the end of his life by his friend Maria Fellinger. It was to be the last photograph of Brahms. He was seriously ill with cancer and died on 3 April, 1897.

Archiv fur Kunst und Geschichte, Berlin

Following Brahms's death, his friends at Gmunden (with whom he had spent many happy summers) transformed their house into an affectionate memorial to him (left). Notice the portrait of the composer on the house's façade.

COMPOSER'S LIFE

Brahms and Clara Schumann

Brahms never married, although he was certainly interested in women, and since his death his biographers have speculated as to the reasons. One suggestion is that Brahms's experiences when playing in dockland bars near his home left their mark on the sensitive teenager. However, the most likely explanation is that the great love of his life, Clara Schumann, was at first forbidden to him and later refused to marry him. Robert Schumann had proclaimed Brahms's greatness in his journal of music criticism, and the younger man became a firm friend of both Robert and Clara. When Schumann lapsed into insanity and after he died, Clara depended on Brahms: she was forbidden to see her husband and her young admirer visited instead to bring her news of Robert's condition. Brahms and Clara Schumann remained close friends for 40 years – most biographers agree that their love was platonic – until Clara died at the age of 76. Brahms died a few months later, stricken with grief.

COMPOSER'S LIFE

'My sole support'

The infatuation Brahms felt for Clara Schumann developed over many years into a deep and lasting friendship, which, despite its 'purity', was not always comfortably platonic.

In September 1853, a young musician arrived in Düsseldorf with a letter of introduction to Robert Schumann – at that time not only one of the greatest living composers, but also one of the leading figures of influence in the musical world. The young man was Johannes Brahms, the second child of a poor Hamburg family.

A batch of compositions that he had sent the master only months earlier had been returned unopened, so that it was with some trepidation that Brahms approached Schumann's house. Moreover, Schumann was by this time under considerable mental stress as a result of his illness (now thought to be the tertiary stage of syphilis), and was known to be morose and uncommunicative.

However, Brahms's reception was immediate and whole-hearted. Sitting down at the piano in the house in the Grabenstrasse, Brahms began to play one of his own pieces, when Schumann interrupted him by saying 'Clara must hear this too.' Returning to the room with his wife he told her: 'Clara, you're now going to hear music such as you've never heard before.'

The experience must have been overwhelming for the young composer; indeed, it was to change his life. Not only was his career to take a dramatic turn – Schumann publicly hailed Brahms as a genius – but Brahms was to become intensely involved with Schumann's wife, Clara, in a relationship that has intrigued biographers ever since.

Recording the meeting in her diary, Clara noted that everything Brahms had written was full of great emotional intensity, consummate in form and brimming over with imagination.

When Brahms and Clara Schumann (below) met in 1853, they felt an immediate rapport, which, for Brahms, soon developed into a passionate form of heroine-worship. Fourteen years his senior, Clara was the epitome of the unobtainable beloved, a central theme in Romantic literature and art (below left).

Bildarchiv Preussischer Kulturbesitz

The Mansell Collection

Edimedia

Brahms's childhood and early teenage years were happy enough, though marred by impoverished circumstances. To contribute to his family's income he had to sing and play the piano in the dockside taverns of Hamburg to audiences of sailors and prostitutes. These experiences of harbour and street life (above) are thought to have contributed to his shyness with women.

A desperate infatuation

As soon as he set foot in the Schumann household, Brahms felt at home. There were books, there was music, there was stimulating conversation. Above all, there were the strength and serenity of Clara, a virtuoso pianist of the highest calibre, a champion of her husband's music, a devoted wife and mother shortly to give birth to her eighth child. And although she was 14 years his senior, Clara was still an attractive woman of 34.

Brahms fell wildly, deeply in love. And it was Clara in all these aspects that he loved. He must have been moved by the way she managed to combine her art with her responsibilities as a mother, and by the unselfish and exemplary way in which she put her husband first. He put Clara high on a pedestal. He worshipped her, but she was firmly out of reach.

Tragic developments

On 28 October, barely a month after Brahms had met the Schumanns, Schumann printed an historic editorial in his magazine *Neue Zeitschrift für Musik*. It was entitled *Neue Bahnen* (New paths), and in it he declared that Brahms was the 'new force' in music. Brahms immediately wrote expressing his gratitude:

Revered master, You have made me so extremely happy that I cannot attempt to express my thanks in words. May God grant that my works will soon be able to prove to you how much your love and kindness have uplifted and inspired me.

Neue Bahnen was to be Schumann's last piece of criticism. His condition was worsening all the time. The baton fell from his fingers as he was trying to conduct. He heard music continually – some made by angels, some made by devils. He had attacks of hysteria and feared he might harm his wife and children. On 27 February 1854, he tried to commit suicide by throwing himself into the Rhine, but was rescued by two fishermen. He begged to be taken to a mental asylum, and eventually his doctors saw that no other course was possible. Since it was felt that seeing his wife might aggravate his condition, Clara was forbidden to visit him until just before his death two years later. These were to be the hardest months of her life.

'God's Consolation'

During this time Brahms's love meant everything to her. When her children were old enough to understand, she felt it necessary to explain the enormous value she placed on their relationship:

God sends a consolation to everyone, however unhappy he may be and we must rejoice at this fact. I had you, of course, but then you were quite small. You hardly knew your beloved father and you were still too young to feel any profound grief. During those terrible years you could bring me no consolation. Hopes, yes, but they hardly sufficed at such moments. And then Johannes Brahms came along. Your father loved and respected him more than any other man in the world. He came as a faithful friend to share my unhappiness; he fortified my aching heart, raised my spirits and solaced my soul as best he could. He was, in fact, a friend in the most complete sense of the word and he was my sole support.

Brahms had already declared his love for her by comparing himself to a prince from the *Arabian Nights*. He wrote:

Would to God that I were allowed this day instead of writing to you to repeat to you with my own lips that I am dying of love for you. Tears prevent me from saying more!

Despite the playful mood of this piece of gentle self-mockery, Clara must have understood her young lover's true feelings. Her own letters to him of this period – about 100 of them – she later insisted on destroying, presumably because they were more ardent than befitted a woman in her situation. But that Brahms's love was returned there can be no doubt.

Although Clara was forbidden to see Schumann, Brahms was a constant and devoted visitor. Schumann's physical and mental powers were shattered. He was by turns quiet and violent. Sometimes he lost control of his limbs, but despite

The Schumann children in about 1855. At the back, from left to right, are Ludwig, who was committed to an asylum for the insane in his 20s, Marie and Elise. On Marie's lap is the baby of the family, Felix, the child whom Robert Schumann never saw. Next to him is Ferdinand, and in the front, Eugénie. Not in the picture are Julie, who had been sent away to live with her grandmother, in Berlin and Emil who died when he was a baby.

As a widow with a large family to support, Clara took up her performing career again. The programme (below) is from a concert given in Gdansk with the violinist Joseph Joachim and Brahms.

this he continued with his activities at the piano. Tactfully Brahms reassured Clara that her husband was in the best hands and at the same time suggested small ways in which she could help him. On 11 June 1854, Clara gave birth to her eighth child, Felix, whom Schumann was never to see.

A week after the birth, Clara was back at the piano, practising for a resumed career. She had turned down offers of financial help from sympathetic admirers of her husband and was proudly determined to support the family herself in the only way she knew, by playing in the concert halls of Europe. She had sent away her third daughter, Julie, to stay with her mother in Berlin, but the problem of the other surviving six children remained. So Brahms moved into Clara's house in Düsseldorf so that he could look after them while she was away.

A lively companion

The arrangement seems to have suited Brahms and the children equally well. His letters show this:

They seem to grow merrier and stronger every day. I have put away a large bag of sweets and they have to earn every one of them by hard work. They even have to wrestle with each other for them.

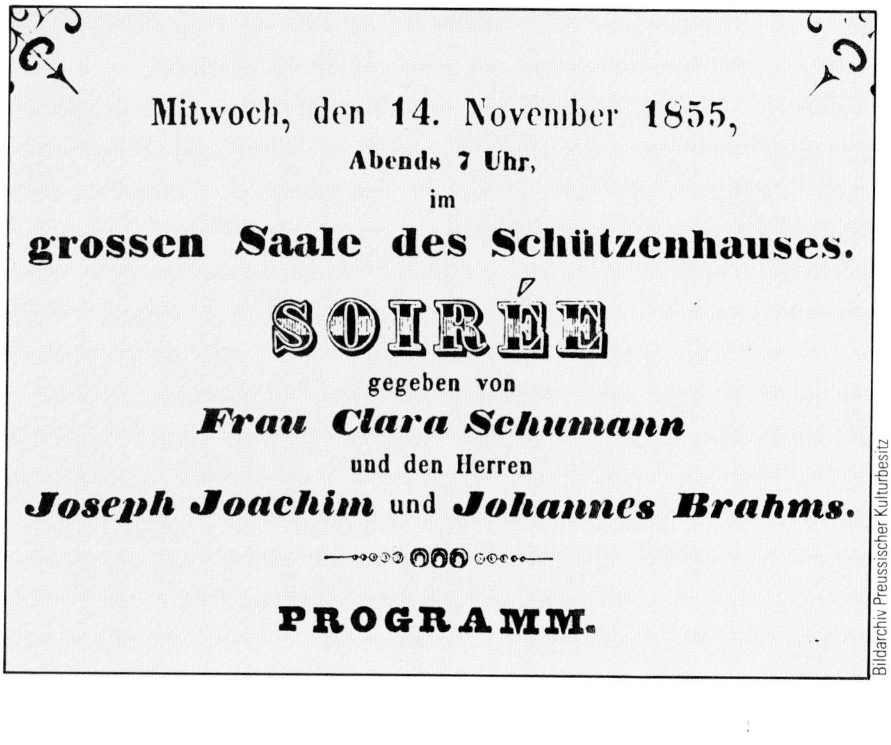

Mitwoch, den 14. November 1855,

Abends 7 Uhr,

im

grossen Saale des Schützenhauses.

SOIRÉE

gegeben von

Frau Clara Schumann

und den Herren

Joseph Joachim und Johannes Brahms.

PROGRAMM.

Bildarchiv Preussischer Kulturbesitz

John Ritchie 'A Summer Day in Hyde Park'. Museum of London

In 1856 Clara visited England on the first of her many concert tours there. She frequently stayed near Hyde Park (above) and despite the grumbles confided to her diary about the inability of English audiences to distinguish good from indifferent performances, she developed an affection for the English countryside and for London's parks.

Julie Schumann (right), the third child of Clara's large brood. Brahms displayed such a particular interest in her, and seemed so disturbed when her engagement was announced, that Clara suspected the composer harboured more than fatherly feelings towards her daughter. Julie was very delicate in health and in 1872 she died of TB.

And he joined in all their activities with childlike enthusiasm:

The principal point is that I have once more acquired a passion for jumping. You would be very surprised, I can jump very well and for a long time, at least twice as far as my height, and very high.

In February 1856, Brahms tried to persuade Clara to accept money from a fund set up to help her so that she need not embark on 'the dangerous journey to England' where she was planning a concert tour. When she remained adamant, he wrote

I have often thought – how often I cannot say – of joining you. But I was afraid it might be regarded as improper, for everything gets into the papers.

Clara was very conscious of wagging tongues, and after Schumann's death at the end of July in that year, it was decided that Brahms should leave the household. He was with Clara at the end; and was one of the pallbearers at the funeral. When the time came for him to leave for Hamburg, Clara accompanied him to the railway station. She was distraught: 'It was like another funeral', she wrote.

A love from afar

Brahms sent her a stream of urgent letters. 'My love for you is indescribable.' 'Send me news of you, as it is my greatest joy. Farewell, my dearest beloved.' Clara did not dampen these fires of passion – after all, she needed his love and support more than ever, but though she wrote back with warmth, she never let Brahms forget her union with Robert.

And this is how it was to remain. It was almost as if Clara, too, had left the world behind and wedded herself to her music. Her letters are full of it. Though her concert tours were supposedly undertaken solely to support her family, there is, however, very little mention of her children, and they must sorely have missed the lively companionship of Brahms.

In fact she only speaks of her children when disaster befalls them and there were to be many tragedies among the Schumann children. Emil died as a baby. Ludwig was committed to an insane asylum in his 20s. Julie, always frail, died leaving two young children. Ferdinand was crippled by rheumatism and died leaving a wife and three young children. (Brahms offered to support them but Clara preferred to do it alone.) Felix, probably the most gifted of all, died of tuberculosis aged 25. All this Clara bore with characteristic fortitude.

By now Brahms had realized that his love was hopeless and he had to come to terms with it. In a strange way he was helped by Clara's own bereavement. 'You have taught me and are every day teaching me evermore to recognise and to marvel at what love, attachment and self-denial are,' he wrote to her. And he goes on to add:

Passions are not natural to mankind, they are always exceptions or excrescence. The man in whom they overstep the limits should regard himself as an invalid and seek a medicine for his life and his health.

An enduring friendship

Widowed at 36, Clara lived and worked until she was 77. Throughout this 40 years Brahms remained her closest friend, offering her love, advice and sympathy, as well as the money she declined. They had one or two misunderstandings, usually because Clara misinterpreted Brahms's solicitude for her as an impertinent reference to her advancing age: Brahms was sometimes rather tactless when trying to persuade her to slow down. Their worst misunderstanding came when Brahms published a manuscript by Schumann that they had previously agreed should not be made public because Clara felt it was unworthy of him. Clara was bitterly insulted and for almost two years she stopped inviting him to her house. On her 73rd birthday, Brahms wrote movingly to heal the rift:

Permit a poor outcast to tell you today that he always thinks of you with the same respect, and out of the fullness of his heart wishes you, whom he holds dearer than anyone on earth, all that is good, desirable and beautiful . . .

And with the letter he enclosed a group of intimate miniatures for the piano that were within the range of Clara's by now limited powers (she suffered from rheumatism in her hands and arms and had sustained several painful falls). She was overjoyed and pronounced them 'Full of poetry, passion, sentiment, [and] emotion'.

There was never anyone in Brahms's life who could take Clara's place in his heart. Clara encouraged him to look for a wife, but probably more out of a sense of guilt-tinged duty than from inclination. When in the summer of 1858 he met Agathe Siebold, a vivacious girl of his own age, Clara could not bear to be in their company. But she need not have worried; though Brahms was attracted and the lady very much in love, he told her he could not face the fetters of marriage.

The only other love in his life appears to have been Clara's daughter Julie. And she was as unattainable as her mother. In 1869, Julie was staying with her mother in Frankfurt and Brahms took lodgings in a house nearby. Julie had fallen in love with an Italian count. The tension between her and Brahms was unbearable. Clara noted in her diary:

Johannes is a changed man. He seldom drops by and then shows himself taciturn even towards Julie, whom he formerly treated with such affection. Could it be that he truly loved her?

His long and deep friendship with Clara ended when she died in the spring of 1896. Beside himself, Brahms rushed from Bad Ischl to attend her funeral in Bonn. Later that year he became ill, his condition rapidly deteriorated and he died in April 1897 – only a year after Clara.

Clara (below) once described her prowess as a musician to Brahms as 'My art . . . my most faithful and trusty friend'. Indeed her talent was more than a consolation, for it was the basis of her income. In later years, however, she was plagued by rheumatism and underwent treatment on several occasions.

Archiv für Kunst und Geschichte

COMPOSER'S LIFE

The 'New Music' controversy

Today, when composers like Liszt and Wagner are amongst those established composers whose works are revered, it is difficult to imagine a time when they and their supporters were seen as rebels – untalented, unmusical rebels at that – against the hallowed forms of music set by Beethoven. Liszt and Wagner did not reject the greatness of Beethoven, but they believed that music should change and develop; their opponents, led by Robert Schumann, wanted to keep music within the Classical idiom. Brahms was very much a traditionalist – unlike Liszt, he saw music as an abstract art, not as a vehicle for self-expression – but in many ways he was a reluctant partisan and was often dragged into controversy by the extremes of his supporters. With hindsight, of course, modern listeners know that both sides in the controversy were led by composers who in their different ways were masters of great music.

COMPOSER'S LIFE

'The very negation of art'

Passions ran high in Germany over the future of music after the death of Beethoven. When rival camps of musicians were formed Brahms was forced reluctantly to carry the torch for his side.

)uring much of Brahms's working life a controversy aged in Germany over the direction that modern nusic should take. On the one side were the advocates of the 'New Music', led by Liszt and Wagner; on the other the devotees of the more traditional approach who looked to Mendelssohn and Schumann as their eroes and regarded Brahms as their champion, hough Brahms himself was always quite unwilling to dopt this role.

In the early days the respective headquarters of the ival camps were the Leipzig Conservatory, founded y Mendelssohn in 1843 and with Schumann as the rst professor of composition, and the court of Veimar where Liszt was musical director in the 1840s nd 50s. Both sides, incidentally, saw themselves as he heirs to Beethoven but whereas Liszt at Weimar imed to extend and explore the language he had equeathed, those at Leipzig were content to work vithin it.

The rivalry between the two camps was building up o its first climax when Brahms, aged 20, played for chumann in 1853. The reaction of the older musician vas ecstatic: 'He is a performer of genius who can nake of the piano an orchestra. In him we welcome a trong champion.'

iszt and Brahms

iszt had also had his eye on the young Brahms and had oped to recruit him to his group of disciples when he young musician arrived in Weimar in 1853 on his rst concert tour with the Hungarian violinist Reményi. le received them both extremely affably and as a reat favour performed a selection of his own works or them.

However, the encounter was not auspicious. 3rahms, it seems, failed to respond to the honour bestowed on him by Europe's most famous pianist with the enthusiasm that had been expected. Liszt may well have been offended, while Reményi, embarrassed by his companion's discourtesy and anxious to secure the great man's approval, broke off his partnership with Brahms.

At the age of 20, Brahms (below) played for Schumann, who was quick to herald him as 'champion' of his musical faction at Leipzig.

Bildarchiv Preussischer Kulturbesitz

In this caricature, Eduard Hanslick, the influential music critic who was vigorously opposed to the attitudes of Wagner, Liszt and their followers, places Brahms high on a pedestal (left). In reality, Brahms did not relish the role of hero, although he sympathized with Hanslick's views.

Liszt was certainly one of the most sensational performers ever to sit before a keyboard and undoubtedly the most dramatic. Years earlier Schumann himself had come under the spell:

The beautiful illuminated hall, the glow of candlelight, the handsomely dressed audience – all elevated the mind, and then the daemon began to stir in Liszt . . . until he had enmeshed every member of the audience with his art and could do with them as he willed.

But though he dazzled, many serious-minded musicians of the old school regretted Liszt's willingness to let the showman run away with him. Clara Schumann, Robert's wife and herself an outstanding pianist, was 'carried away' by his performance of Schubert and conceded his mastery of the instrument, but remained uneasy. 'One always feels as if some devilish force were sweeping one along.' Moreover she despised his showman's tactics – 'petty coquetries' she called them and found his own works 'odious'.

Brahms, too, was temperamentally out of tune with the flashy bravura that Liszt often indulged in as a performer and had no sympathy at all with the principles of composition advanced by the New Music. His own work was revered by the well-known music critic Eduard Hanslick because it was 'unified' and 'clearly set out'. The famous conductor Hans von Bülow liked to refer to Brahms's First and Second Symphonies as the 'Tenth' and 'Eleventh' because in his view they carried on the classical tradition of Beethoven. For this reason Brahms's music today is sometimes described as 'classical-romantic'.

Liszt was characteristically contemptuous of this approach which seemed to him typical of the hidebound attitudes which he believed governed most of German musical life. Although he acknowledged the debt to Beethoven and the inspiration to be gained from him, he saw this as a starting point, not as a framework:

Mary Evans Picture Library

Liszt (above) whose brilliant but showy piano playing antagonized many traditionalists.

Robert Harding Picture Library

A model of one of the elaborate contemporary stage sets for Wagner's **Die Meistersinger,** ***first performed in Munich in 1868 with Hans von Bülow (who later sided with Brahms) conducting.***

Mary Evans Picture Library

Jealous of his own position in music, Wagner (above) detested comparisons with Brahms.

Although a hundred other cities may stop at Beethoven (though while he lived they much preferred Haydn and Mozart), there is no reason why we in Weimar should. No doubt in this year 1855, there is nothing better than to respect, admire and study the illustrious dead, but why should we not also sometimes live with the living? That is the implication of the movement of which Weimar is the centre.

The dispute

The controversy between the two schools of thought was not a simple one. Liszt himself certainly admired the old masters, and Schumann founded his journal *Neue Zeitschrift* in 1834 precisely to combat the philistinism of conventional music lovers and promote what he saw as the best among the new generation of composers.

Both sides were devoted to modern music; the argument was over the course it should take. In the 1840s Mendelssohn had made his newly founded Conservatory at Leipzig into Germany's foremost institution of music. It was founded on sound disciplines of orchestral practice and grounded upon classical rules of composition. A generation of musicians grew up in the atmosphere of Leipzig.

Whereas the group originated in Leipzig admired the classical ideals of orderliness and perfection and held that music was essentially abstract art and not simply the vehicle for personal self-expression, the Liszt-Wagner movement believed that music could be the outward manifestation of character. While the Brahmsians claimed to work within the classical idiom, the Weimar school championed every opportunity for the expression of the passions. To them the music of that arch-Romantic Berlioz was an inspiration and they pursued new directions of their own, seeking to loosen the fetters of conventional harmony and insisting that musical form should be stretched so that it could embody poetic ideas.

The shadow of Wagner

If the time should come when everyone wrote in the style of Wagner our audiences would infallibly end in the mad house; and should his manner of conducting music ever win unchallenged sway in our orchestras, the leaders, strings and wind players would become fellow inmates.

So Eduard Hanslick, staunch champion of Brahms, reviewed a concert conducted by Wagner in 1872. Wagner for his part regarded Hanslick as the archetypal reactionary and used him as the model for the pedant Hans Beckmesser in *Die Meistersinger*.

When he first read the score of Wagner's opera *Tannhäuser* Schumann scathingly observed: 'a brilliant fellow with audacious ideas, but barely able to set down (let alone think out) a four bar phrase beautifully or even correctly. He is one of those fellows who have not learned their harmony lessons.' Schumann was generous enough to withdraw something of this when he saw a performance shortly afterwards: 'On stage everything strikes one differently' he remarked, but his suspicion and dislike of these new trends in music remained.

Such generosity was certainly never part of Wagner's character. Brahms, who had helped the copyists writing out the parts for *Die Meistersinger* in Vienna, felt the lash of his tongue on many an occasion. Writing to the publisher Schott to urge him to publish

Mary Evans Picture Library

The Ring, *Wagner's most important opera, is an allegory describing a very different power struggle to the one which took place between the warring musical camps. The conflict is between dwarfs, giants and gods. In the story the dwarf Alberich (left) steals the Rhinegold from the Rhinemaidens to forge the all-powerful ring that bestows upon its wearer the ability to change shape and form.*

Historisches Museum der Stadt Wien

Students gather to talk over revolutionary ideas in Vienna in the troubled year of 1848 (above). The revolutions forced the politically-minded Wagner into hiding, while providing Brahms with musical influences from fleeing refugees.

some Italian chamber music, Wagner sneered: 'I would expect these works to have an outstanding success after the tedium of recent German chamber music – Brahms etc.' When a piano transcription of Brahms's *Triumphlied* was played to him he dismissed it as a work without creative urge or sincerity – 'all Handel, Mendelssohn and Schumann swaddled in leather'.

Although Brahms rejected 'the silly tone that musicians here in Vienna use against Wagner', he was not above the occasional measured outburst himself. In one of his letters to Clara Schumann he wrote:

In everything else I attempt I step on the heels of my predecessors and am embarrassed. But Wagner would not hinder me at all from proceeding with the greatest pleasure to the writing of an opera.

Wagner's hostility to Brahms lay partly in the fac that as the careers of the two men progressed the were naturally seen by the public as rivals, as the tw great figures of contemporary music, which Wagne was unable to tolerate. He believed that no-one wa his equal and sometimes, one feels, barely rate Brahms as a musician at all. Not only did he conside his compositions tedious, he thought Brahms lackin in the intuitive 'feel' for music essential for an composer of genius. After hearing one of Bellini operas, which he judged poor in terms of musica craftsmanship, Wagner nevertheless confessed hi admiration for the 'passion and emotion' which la behind it and went on: 'I learned something from thi that Messrs Brahms and Co. could never learn and pu it into my melody.'

His admiration for the philosopher Schopenhaue led Wagner to send him a copy of *The Ring* which h had, of course, written himself and of which he wa inordinately proud. Regrettably, the sage made n response whatever to the gesture by his admirer Wagner peevishly compared this to the off-hand wa in which the great Goethe had treated the poet Kleis and declared that Schopenhauer 'should have hailed me as joyfully as Schumann did Brahms. But that seem to happen only amongst the donkeys'.

After all this it can be imagined the fury with whic Wagner in 1879 heard the news that the University o Breslau had awarded Brahms an honorary doctorate

Liszt was considered to be as great a virtuoso on the piano as Paganini on the violin. He is seen here (right) playing to the violinist and other friends including the composer Berlioz and the writer George Sand.

'he citation only rubbed salt in the wound for it lared to describe the recipient as 'the principal epresentative of serious music now in Germany'. Vagner rushed into print with an outright attack on Brahms in a piece entitled *Concerning Poetry and Composition.* By the time he had finished, the reader vas left in no doubt that Wagner considered that Germany's principal representative of serious music', wooden Johannes', as he scathingly termed him, was qualified in neither of the arts in the title.

'he man in the middle

Younger than Wagner by 20 years, Brahms was always, o some extent, the unwilling figurehead of the anti-Wagner faction. By and large he wished to hold himself aloof from this controversy. It was for him a natter of indifference whether an artist thought in progressive or conservative terms, and though he lisliked Wagner's methods he recognized his genius.

Moreover, Brahms was never as politically committed as Wagner had been in his youth. Brought up in he poor quarter of the city of Hamburg and from an early age working in the quayside taverns as a bar pianist, Brahms always felt himself to be a man of the people. His admiration for and friendship with the valtz king Johann Strauss reflected this allegiance musically – but his political awareness was never raised.

The Year of Revolutions, 1848, which shook Europe and caught up the 35-year-old Wagner, affected Hamburg and the 15-year-old Brahms only marginally. Among the thousands of refugees driven on to the roads in the great upheaval were many Hungarians, among them gypsy musicians who passed through Hamburg and fascinated the young Brahms with their art. His encounter with the Hungarian violinist Reményi, however, was more important. Forced into exile by his participation in the events of '48, Reményi fled first to America and then returned to Europe, landing at the port of Hamburg. He and Brahms struck up an immediate partnership and in 1853 began a series of tours which took them to the great centres such as Weimar, exposing them to the 'New Music' and precipitating Brahms into the controversy which was to dog him intermittently for the rest of his life.

Liszt at this time was beginning to attract hostile comments from the courtly society at Weimar. His good friend Wagner had been forced to flee Saxony because of his revolutionary pamphleteering and support for the rising in Dresden in May 1849. Liszt assisted him in his flight. For Liszt and Wagner, the break with musical conventions was part of a lifestyle which also rejected social and political conventions.

Insults and treachery

Liszt, musical director at Weimar for more than a decade, had used his position to promote modern music. He even included the operas of Robert Schumann and, though the two men were to draw apart

Staatsbibliothek, Berlin/Robert Harding Picture Library

The brilliant young violinist, Joachim, a warm friend of Brahms's, is accompanied by the famous pianist Clara Schumann (above).

Bildarchiv Preussischer Kulturbesitz

Brahms (left) towards the end of his life. By this time the wranglings and bitterness over the musical debate seemed very remote.

The 'New Music' embodied in the works of Wagner was, to the traditionalists, ear-splitting. In this cruel caricature the point is taken literally.

The Mansell Collection

***The distinguished pianist and world-famous conductor Hans von Bülow (above) recognized the genius of both Wagner and Brahms. He is caricatured here conducting Wagner's* Tristan und Isolde.**

in their ideas, Liszt, as Clara Schumann was later to write to Brahms, never made any personal attack on Robert. It was not so with Wagner 'who did not scruple to speak in the most contemptuous manner about Robert, Mendelssohn and all of you'. Both Liszt and Wagner demanded loyalty from their followers. Liszt gathered round him a guard of young shock troops to promote his ideas. They thronged his house at Weimar's Altenburg and called themselves 'the Moors' ('Murls' in German slang). The badge of 'Murlship' implied total allegiance to the principles of the New Music and total allegiance to Liszt.

One or two of the Murls generally accompanied Liszt on his journeys. In 1853 the whole group journeyed to the exiled Wagner in Switzerland and then to Leipzig to support a Berlioz concert. At Liszt's own concerts they formed the core of the clique which guaranteed the audience applause for his works. Brahms was no sycophant, and this atmosphere of hero-worship was as objectionable to him as the ideas behind the New Music.

Among the keenest of Liszt's devotees for a time wa[s] the Hungarian-born violinist and composer Josep[h] Joachim. A child prodigy, he made his concert début aged 12, at Leipzig in 1843, with Clara Schumann an[d] Mendelssohn. Then from 1849–50 he shifted hi[s] allegiance to Weimar, accepting Liszt's invitation t[o] become concert master of the orchestra there. Fou[r] years later he took a post in Hanover. His adherence t[o] the New Music weakened and in the mid-1850s h[e] wrote to Clara Schumann:

Liszt's compositions are a vulgar abuse of the sacre[d] forms of music . . . one whom I once thought to be a mighty spirit striving to return to God I now realize to be merely a cunning contriver of effects. You wer[e] right Madame Schumann.

Although she had less personal animosity for Lisz[t] than for Wagner, Clara had rejected his music. Describing to Brahms a concert in which Liszt's *Prometheus* had been followed by Mozart's Symphon[y] ɪo. 40 in G minor, she quoted the words of their ıutual friend the critic Hanslick. 'When the first notes f the Mozart were heard, they were "like a soft breeze ıddenly wafting into a room reeking with fumes".' assions were running high. Some of the 'Murls' onsidered Joachim's desertion of Weimar and Liszt as ttle better than treachery. The violinist's clarification f his position was belated but quite explicit when it id come. He wrote to his one-time hero:

our music is entirely antagonistic to me. It is pposed to everything which the spirits of our great nes have nourished in my heart. Were I ever to be eprived of all that I honour and cherish in their reations, what for me is the very essence of music erself, your works would not fill a single corner of ıat vast nothingness.

he manifesto

et even the new Joachim did not receive Clara chumann's entirely uncritical approval. In May 1859 ıe wrote to Brahms that she had heard Joachim's *ungarian Concerto* and had found a good deal of it) be distinctly Wagnerian in tone, which 'displeased' er somewhat. The following year, Joachim was a ading sponsor of the manifesto against the New Iusic of the 'futurists', as the Liszt-Wagner faction ometimes liked to call themselves. The signatories, ho described themselves as 'serious and striving ıusicians', included Joachim himself, Bernhard cholz, the Hanoverian court music director, and rahms.

The manifesto castigated the new theories of omposition as 'contrary to the innermost spirit of ıusic' and 'the very negation of art'. It had little npact on its opponents who, using Wagner's own ords, could patronizingly dismiss Brahms as 'the uardian of musical chastity'. Brahms himself, whose ame was the rallying cry for the supporters of the ıanifesto, was hardly its most enthusiastic promoter.

Towards the end of his life, he was to describe anslick's views on Wagner as a blind spot in the great ritic's musical awareness, and his life-long friend lara Schumann almost certainly influenced his pposition to the 'futurists'. Her attitude was npregnable to change. 'I heard *Lohengrin* in Vienna nce,' she wrote in 1859, 'and can see only too easily ow such an opera succeeds in imposing on people.' he innocently admits that the work is so full of omanticism and thrilling situations' that even a ıusician may at times 'forget the horrible music'.

losing the gap

he controversy, conducted in letters, articles and ublic statements and couched in the language of ıusical and artistic debate, stemmed at least in part om the personal rivalries and animosities generated nong the principal protagonists during their youth.

In the hope of reconciling the opposing factions, the eneral German Music Association (Allgemeiner eutscher Musik Verein) had been inaugurated in 861 under the presidency of the musicologist Franz rendel. Schumann's successor as editor of the *Neue eitschrift* and Mendelssohn's Professor of Music istory at Leipzig back in the 40s, he had credentials) act as mediator. But he had shifted the emphasis of chumann's journal towards the Weimar position of iszt and Wagner and so his initiative was met by the ıanifesto against the New Music. Brendel had begun is career as a pianist and was one of the pupils of Clara chumann's father, Friedrich Wieck.

The Mansell Collection

It fell to Gustav Mahler (left) to have the last word in the musical debate that had occupied the time and passions of some of the century's greatest musical talents. Brahms once admitted to Mahler that he thought of himself as the last composer of 'conscious musical integrity'. Mahler pointed to the river by which they were walking and gently asked: 'Is that the last wave?'

Hans von Bülow

Among Wieck's many other distinguished pupils was Hans von Bülow who became an ardent devotee of the New Music.

Deeply impressed by Wagner's tract on *Art and Revolution* and Liszt's performance of *Lohengrin* at Weimar in 1850, von Bülow abandoned his legal studies to devote himself to music. Liszt assured his parents that the 21-year-old was one of the 'greatest musical organisms' of his generation and the young man completed his initiation into the New Music under the tutelage of Wagner, later conducting some of the most brilliant premières of his operas at Munich under the composer's direction.

Over the next 40 years he established himself as one of Germany's greatest conductors and by his marriage to Liszt's daughter Cosima in 1857 seemed to seal his alliance with the Weimar school. Unfortunately the marriage slowly broke up as Cosima became infatuated with Wagner. After divorce, and to the fury of her father, Cosima married the composer.

After a few years in Florence to nurse his bruised ego, von Bülow returned to German musical life. He never abandoned his admiration for Wagner as a composer but, as director of the court orchestra at Meiningen in the 1880s, he became a great champion of Brahms's music.

In many ways Brahms was the reluctant hero, the traditionalist throughout the turbulent years of controversy. He suffered abuse from Wagner and the often unsought partisanship of his own supporters. He never accepted that the poetic idea could be the basis of the musical form. But he was too much the musician not to recognize the achievements of his rivals, no matter how much he might reject their intellectual rationale. Throughout the decades of simmering debate, Brahms remained true to himself, however much others might wish to blazon his name on banners in a battle which was of their making, not of his.

Listener's guide

Any analysis of the life and times of a great composer cannot ignore his music, and the Listener's Guide *examines in detail some of Brahms's greatest and best-known works: the Violin Concerto in D, his Second Piano Concerto and his First Symphony – often called 'Beethoven's Tenth' for its fidelity to that great composer's tradition. The sections on specific aspects of musical development (for example, the inspiration that Brahms and other composers drew from gypsy music, and the changes in piano technology during the 19th century) can be read, along with the descriptions of the pieces of music, as an examination of Brahms's musical genius. However, for the fullest appreciation of this great composer's music, the programme notes are better read before going to a live performance or while listening to the recorded music. Suggestions for further listening are given in the text, and the short descriptions of the lives and works of notable contemporary composers suggest alternative areas for further study.*

LISTENER'S GUIDE

Violin Concerto in D, op. 77

Brahms's Violin Concerto is one of his supreme achievements. The brilliance of the solo part, which combines lyrical beauty with shear vitality, is matched by Brahms's careful and masterly scoring.

Brahms's Violin Concerto is one of the great examples of its kind, worthy of standing side by side with the one by Beethoven, which he so admired and which shares the same key – D major.

It illustrates his deep understanding of the form of the classical 'concerto' — a word which comes from the Italian *concertare* – to strive with – expressing the conflict, or discussion, leading to greater understanding, between the soloist and the orchestra.

The contemporary critic, Hans von Bülow, said, on first hearing the work, that whereas Max Bruch had written a concerto *for* the violin, Brahms had written a concerto *against* the violin. This epigram was later revised by Bronislav Huberman – who had played the Concerto when only 12 years old to a delighted Brahms – to express more accurately Brahms's achievement:

Brahms's concerto is neither against *the violin, nor* for *violin* against *orchestra; but it is a concerto* for *violin* against *orchestra – and the violin wins.*

That it does so is in a large measure due to the fact that it was written for, and with the help of, the greatest violinist of the day – Joseph Joachim. Personalities and friendships inspired many of Brahms's works. The First Symphony and Second Piano Concerto recall the tragic death of his close friend, the composer Robert Schumann, and the German Requiem the death of his mother. This Concerto celebrates Brahms's long and sometimes strained friendship with Joachim, to whom it is dedicated.

Joseph Joachim

In 1852, when Brahms was 20, he had met a Hungarian-Jewish violinist, Edward Reményi, who loved to play Hungarian gypsy music – the influence of which can be heard in the last movement, written *alla zingarese* (in gypsy style). Together, they travelled on a concert tour, during which Reményi hoped they would meet his friend Joachim, to whom he wanted to introduce Brahms.

Brahms had been so deeply impressed by Joachim's interpretation of Beethoven's Violin Concerto, which he had heard in his native Hamburg five years before, that when they met he felt so in awe in the presence of his idol that he was too shy to speak. Instead, he played a sonata. Joachim was bowled over by the 'power and originality' of the composition, and by the 'tender and imaginative, free and fiery' nature of his playing. The two became close friends. They both composed, and criticized each other's compositions – a habit they kept up all their lives; when not together they would send each other musical exercises by post.

Joachim had repeatedly urged Brahms to write a violin concerto – partly as a tribute to their mutual friend Schumann, who had composed a violin concerto during the misery of his last illness, but which Joachim had felt kinder to his reputation to leave unpublished.

When Brahms finally completed his Concerto at Pörtschach in 1878, he sent the violin solo part of the first movement to Joachim with the request:

After having written it out, I really don't know what you will make of the solo part alone. It was my intention, of course, that you should correct it, not sparing the quality of composition, and that, if you thought it not worth scoring, you would say so. I shall be satisfied if you will mark those parts which are difficult, awkward, or impossible to play. The whole affair is in four movements.

By return, Joachim replied:

It gives me great pleasure to know that you are composing a violin concerto – in four movements too! I have had a good look at what you sent me, but without the full score one can't say much. I can however make out most of it, and there is a lot of good music in it, but whether it can be played with comfort in a hot concert hall remains to be seen. Can we spend a couple of days together?

Joachim was summoned to Pörtschach, and, as described by Claude Rostand in his book on Brahms, arrived on Brahms's doorstep at the beginning of September. Both men probably realized that the discussions would take a lively turn: indeed, Brahms listened attentively to Joachim's suggestions concerning the composition as a whole, but, when his friend started criticizing details of instrumental technique, he showed incredible stubborness. The discussions took on epic proportions. Brahms would not shift an inch. He raised his voice, stamped with rage and refused to see Joachim's viewpoint. And so it went on for several days, each emerging in the morning to do battle again. Gradually, both men conceded a little ground. Brahms agreed to correct the solo part, inserting Joachim's suggested revisions, after the violinist had pointed out the advantages. However, he stood firm in refusing to depart from his basic idea.

After Joachim's departure, the discussions continued by post, and Brahms eventually dedicated the concerto to him: 'You will think twice before you ask me for another Concerto! It is a good thing that your name is on the cover; you are more or less responsible for the Solo Violin part.' Moreover, Brahms paid Joachim the great compliment of allowing him to compose the *cadenza* – the extended virtuoso solo passage for violin towards the end of the first movement.

However, he was worried that Joachim might make the violin part too demanding for a lesser player, and hesitated to publish it. Joachim kept the manuscript score, and played the work frequently. He first performed it on January 1, 1879 in Leipzig, where it received a lukewarm reception; but it met with greater success in England, where it was performed in London at the Crystal Palace in February 1879. Joachim had admitted all along that he could only assess the work fairly under concert conditions, and, as a result, he continued to suggest amendments which might make the work easier for the soloist to perform. The Concerto's popularity grew, and in 1888 Joachim was able to write enthusiastically: 'I have been playing your fiddle concerto, and have already given it in

Manchester to an audience of 3000, and next in Liverpool and Bradford, in each case with Hallé's orchestra.'

Creative summer holidays

When Brahms came to write his Violin Concerto, he was in the high summer of his creative life. He was now an esteemed and wealthy musician, thanks largely to the astute management of his business affairs by his publisher, Simrock. He had settled in Vienna, where he enjoyed the theatre, a wide circle of friends, and good food, drink, and cigars – as his stoutening figure walking the Prater testified. But most of all, he enjoyed his summer holidays, when he could escape to do some serious composing. He chose the lakes and mountains, where he could renew his creative energy with the long walks that he, like Beethoven before him, found such an inspiration, amid majestic panoramas. Choosing where to go each summer became an enjoyable and absorbing obsession.

In 1876 it was Sassnitz, on the island of Rügen in the Baltic, where he went swimming with his friend, the singer George Herschel, diving down to the bottom of the lake, with eyes wide open, looking for pebbles.

In 1877 he discovered Pörtschach on the Wörthersee, in Carinthia – then an Alpine province of Austria – where he wrote his Second Symphony and in the following year, his Violin Concerto. He described it as a place 'where so many melodies fly about that one must be careful not to tread on them.' It was easy to recognize the benign influence of the landscape on his work. His close friend, the great surgeon Theodor Billroth, commented on the Symphony: 'That symphony is like blue heavens, the murmur of springs, sunshine, and cool green shadows!'

The same poetic qualities are to be found in the Violin Concerto.

Programme notes

First movement – Allegro non troppo. Cadenza – Joachim.

In order to understand the scale and complexity of the immense first movement, often hailed, together with the finale of the Fourth Symphony, as Brahms's most masterly large scale achievement, it is necessary to understand the need of a composer following in the footsteps of Bach and Beethoven, to break down, develop, and elaborate the often simple melodic themes that hold the work together. 'Why can't he leave such a good tune alone?' one might be tempted to ask, on a first hearing. But by breaking a theme down into its constituent elements, and playing with them, Brahms rearranges the 'building blocks' of his work to explore the very structure of the musical language he is using.

Structure is all important to Brahms, as opposed, for example, to his contemporary romantic, Liszt; it is a container for his romantic emotions. Strict musical form and logic, as instilled in him by his teacher Marxsen, was the discipline, the architecture he needed to keep the expression of ideas from becoming mere self-expression. The architecture of this grand and imposing first movement may be compared to the edifice of a cathedral, revealing in its arches and buttresses the strength that holds it together, and makes possible the piercing beauties of its glass and statuary.

The first theme, (a), with its upward and downward curve, mirrors itself like a mountain reflected in a lake whose calm waters are soon to be disturbed. The serenity of this theme – played on violas, cellos, bassoons, and strings, and rounded off by the addition of horns – is closely allied to the opening of Brahms's Second Symphony, sometimes called his 'Pastoral', and is a far cry from the stressful openings of his First Symphony and Second Piano Concerto.

The theme leads to a second idea, (b), on the oboe, and a third, (c), written with such masterly compression that the three are made to sound like one continuous theme; but each will be developed independently and contrasted with the others. The third theme, more dramatic than the others, leads to an outburst by the whole orchestra, restating the opening theme, (a), so triumphantly that it assumes

Staatsbibliothek Preussischer Kulturbesitz, Berlin

The Mansell Collection

Brahms wrote the Violin Concerto for his friend, the great violinist Joseph Joachim (far right). He invited Joachim to correct the solo part, asking him to mark any part which was 'difficult, awkward or impossible to play'. After some lively discussion, Joachim amended the score, inserting his corrections in pencil (right).

Leonardo da Vinci 'The Virgin of the Rocks' (detail). Reproduced by courtesy of the Trustees, The National Gallery, London

The timeless, celestial music of the second movement – the Adagio – with its long, lingering melody, is reflected in the beauty and stillness of Leonardo's angel (above).

quite a different character, and makes way for three more themes, similarly linked. These form the 'second subject', or 'sub-plot' of the drama about to be unfolded.

Example 2

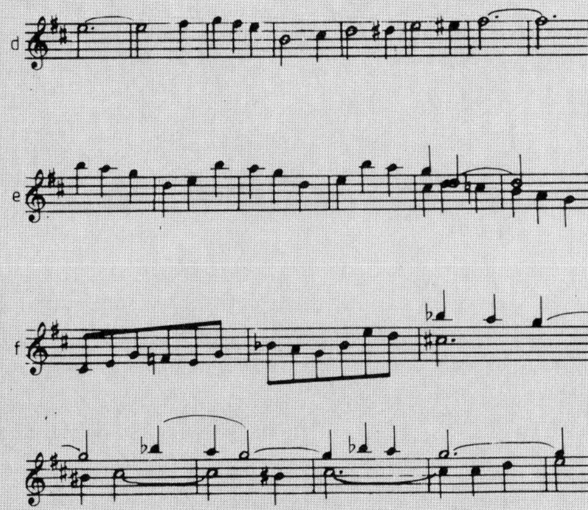

The last of these, (f), rising shyly and only half unfolding, is very important in view of the wonderful way Brahms uses it later in the movement.

The whole cast of 'actors' – all the thematic material – has now been assembled on the stage, and awaits the entry of the 'hero' – the solo violin.

This is a marvellous moment. The orchestra, with falling woodwind, dies down to an expectant hush, and pauses; suddenly, a fanfare sounds, which, with great musical tact, Brahms gives to the strings rather than the brass, where one might have expected it, in order not to upstage or overshadow the solo violin as it makes its entrance. To a roll of drums, the violin strides onto the stage, and with a flourish immediately takes up the argument. It picks up the first theme with so much energy, it manages to transform it almost completely beyond recognition.

The violin hovers, with a lovely viola accompaniment, and trills like a lark flutters its wings to maintain height; then gradually descends to an energetic chord section, which shows how well Brahms understood the dual nature of the violin, using it one moment for a long line of singing melody – or *cantilena* – and the next as a 'fiddle', with all the energy born of dance. When the violin comes to explore the third theme of the second subject, (f), it turns it into a completely new melody. This is a masterstroke of Brahms, bringing what was in the shade to flower in a new light. The melody, with its touching, expressive 'leaps', could only be played by the violin and is a wonderful assertion of the soloist's individuality.

There are many other beauties, too numerous to mention, as the violin continues to question, reinterpret, and transform everything that has already been said by the orchestra. Of particular interest is the way Brahms makes the violin 'tame' the orchestra – so much so, that when it comes to start the development section, the orchestra uses, not its own version of the opening theme, but an agitated variant of the soloist's entry. At times, the violinist uses the bow, as one critic has put it, 'as a rapier against the orchestra, who are now seen as a swarm of adversaries.' Throughout, Brahms continues to show his mastery in 'ringing the changes', getting every shade of meaning and mood out of the same theme.

And so the cadenza is reached. The orchestra – and Brahms – stop for Joachim to display his virtuosity and shed yet another light on what we have already been given.

The short conclusion after the cadenza is one of the most sublime pieces in all music, containing, as Tovey so aptly says, 'some of the tenderest notes ever drawn from a violin.' After climbing to even higher heavens in an ecstasy of contemplation, the violin is gently brought down to earth again by the prodding of horns. The pace imperceptibly quickens, and the great river of music flows out to sea in a triumphant end.

Second movement – Adagio

The Adagio is written with an almost chamber-music sparseness of orchestral texture. Passages for wind instruments alone provide a relaxation from the orchestral weight of the first movement, and give added clarity to the solo violin by freeing it from having to compete with the other stringed instruments in the orchestra.

The beautiful, broad, long, self-mirroring melody is stated on flutes, oboes,

Structure in music was all important to Brahms. The grand architecture of the Violin Concerto can be compared to the edifice of a cathedral (below), where the columns and arches that form its strength make possible the richness and beauty of stained glass and statuary.

David Roberts 'Interior of St. Gommar, Lierre'. Reproduced by permission of the Trustees, The Wallace Collection, London

Understanding music: gypsy music

There is a general, if somewhat unea agreement as to the origins of the gypsi they seem to have originated as a relativ homogenous nomadic people in Northe India. They began to arrive in Euro between the fifth and tenth centuries after lengthy stays in Persia, Turkey ar later and more particularly, Greece. Ove good many centuries after that th largely unco-ordinated wanderings to them slowly throughout Europe and th became an established, if hardly tolerat minority.

The gypsies call themselves 'Rom', t literal translation of which is 'person', 'gypsy man'. The word itself is of Indi origin, as is their language. The actual wo 'gypsy' is not in their language, and is corruption of the English word 'egyptian a clue to both the confusion over th origins and their own tendency to acce misleading myths about themselves.

Consequently, the term 'gypsy mus can only be used as a vague pointer to large and bewilderingly complicated ove lapping of many folk styles and traditio This is chiefly caused by the gypsies' ow preference for relying on aural, rather th written, tradition, and for improvisation.

It is perhaps simplest to break the mus down into a few convenient sub-grou folk music of Hungarian gypsy trib music by gypsies outside Hunga especially Russian; and the musical hybri (or at least some of them!) that resulted.

Plain Hungarian folk-gypsy mus utilizing melodies with largely gyp origins, is almost purely vocal, and is rare accompanied by any musical instrume Both Hungarian and Romany are used these songs. There are thousands of gyp melodies, a great many of which have be luckily preserved by assiduous researche and they basically break down into tw types – slow songs, for laments and oth private expression; and dance-songs.

The songs themselves allow a great de of room for improvisation, which is at t heart of gypsy music. Melodies are dictat largely by the lines of text, and in the slo songs the rhythm is suspended, much the manner of early American negro fie hollers. Even at this stage, with the danc songs in particular, there is a cle influence of Hungarian folk and popul melody, though it is never an order thing, as gypsies have no ritual music. this folk-gypsy music, the only instrumen ever used for accompaniment are t Zither and, occasionally, primitive pe cussion such as a stick on a hollow vesse

Throughout the rest of Europe, differe traditions emerged: in the Balkan stat and Turkey, instrumental ensembl

Composers like Liszt and Brahms were attracted by the energy and excitement of 'gypsy' dance music (above).

evolved using both reed and string instruments, and this usage passed on into Yugoslavia and even parts of southern Hungary later on. Russian gypsies had a music very similar in concept to the Hungarian variety, using vocals which were only occasionally accompanied by stringed instruments. By the 19th century their repertoire was mostly dominated by Russian and Polish folk melodies, and – surprisingly – melodies by contemporary Russian composers.

This last point leads us into the important – and vexed – area of the influence of gypsy music on European composers. It is clear at least that gypsies were playing professionally, in 'gypsy bands' and as soloists, by the middle of the 18th Century, often under the patronage of Hungarian and Austrian noblemen. The music was even then an amalgam of folk music and gypsy stylization, and as their popularity spread towards the end of the century, individual musicians increasingly took lessons in Western music styles and theory, if only at the most basic level.

One of the most crucial developments which helped spread the style through all levels of society in Hungary was the appearance by the close of that century of the *verbunkos,* or recruiting-song: this was a dance performed by soldiers travelling from village to village recruiting for the army, accompanied for the most part by gypsies. Taking basic folk material, the musicians would endeavour to perform the tunes in the most impressive and exciting way possible. Being natural improvisers and embellishers, they evolved a number of ways of heightening the expression of such material which were to prove of enormous influence later on in the 19th century. The appearance of published manuscripts by composers in this 'verbunkos' mode led to the style being increasingly listened to by a whole range of composers.

The new style slowly interacted with the early 19th-century explosion of popular Hungarian art-songs, which itself was greatly encouraged by the appetite of the increasingly dominant Hungarian bourgeoisie for such music. These pieces adapted easily to gypsy interpretation, and by the second half of the century they had been so successfully claimed by gypsy bands, who were then at the zenith of their popular appeal, that most people were content to believe that the melodies used were original gypsy songs!

It was at this stage that composers such as Liszt and Brahms took an intense interest in the melodies and characteristic forms of expression they discovered in the music, and wrote their own compositions,

Brahms was introduced to gypsy music by the Hungarian violinist, Reményi (on left), with whom he toured in his youth.

based (as they thought) on original gypsy material. However, someone such as Liszt, a true romantic who saw the gypsies' music as a wonderful natural expression of man's quest for life and freedom, could never have untangled the complex strands he uncovered. Even so, Liszt should not be dismissed as a mere dilettante, for he took the trouble to write one of the first books on the subject. The hard work and sheer dedication needed for the task was finally given by Bartok and Kodaly in the few years given to this century before the First World War destroyed so much of the folk music of their native land. It is only in their transcriptions and compositions that one can discern the genuine gypsy music that Liszt and Brahms thought they had captured over half a century earlier.

and clarinets, on a bed of horns and bassoons. At its close, the strings join in some hushed, sustained notes, preparing for the violin's entry. All the thematic material has now been assembled for the violin to elaborate on in an exact and wonderfully amplified variation; it takes the theme and expands it by taking two bars over what in the orchestral version took one – giving a most beautiful effect of slowing time to allow for lingering detail.

A conversation now ensues between violin and orchestra. The violin restates the theme, with the orchestra making 'approving' noises; first the flute, and then the horn almost seem to say 'Yes . . . yes . . . we know', sympathetically, encouragingly, as the violin explores the world they have made for it. But once having won the approval of the orchestra, the violin feels free to 'take off', and makes the theme its own, playing it in a way that no other instrument could play it. Brahms, in his usual self-deprecating manner, described this Adagio as 'feeble' when he altered the plan of the work to be in three rather than four movements, writing to Joachim: 'The middle movements are failures. I have written a feeble adagio instead.' However, it contains some of his most celestial music, and it is a measure of his greatness that the movement appears so simple, with a single, singing melody running through it without interruption.

However, the subtlety behind the simplicity can be seen to good advantage in the final section of the movement. When the oboe returns with the opening melody, the violin takes even longer to expand it more lovingly, and then gives an unexplored section of the tune a whole new extension in dialogue with the horns. The music dies away, and the violin, now content to play 'second fiddle' to the orchestra in a spirit of reconciliation, accompanies the fading woodwind. For the very end, Brahms saves a stroke of genius. Then, and only then, he repeats the last section – *codetta,* meaning 'little tail' – of the opening theme. The first chords of the movement, on bassoons and horns, are heard again, and the violin climbs with pointed, staccato notes to a truce.

Third movement – Allegro giocoso, ma non troppo vivace

It is now the violin's turn to start off, having waited patiently in the first two movements for the orchestra to set the scene. With a great flourish, it produces the bouncy opening tune, accompanied by runs on the strings to give it an extra boost. The orchestra does not even question it, but accepts it immediately, relishing the romp, and jumping onto the bandwagon with brass and woodwind. The violinist takes it

The enormous vitality of the final movement, with its joyous, bouncing rhythm, finds a parallel in the Bacchic revelry of Francesco Zuccarelli's painting (right).

Francesco Zuccarelli 'Bacchanal'. Accademia, Venice/Giraudon

a stage further with an incredibly difficult passage of double-stopping – the simultaneous sound of two stopped strings. The marking *ma non troppo vivace,* which qualifies the direction *Allegro giocoso, ma non troppo vivace* (Fast and playful, but not too lively), was probably added by Joachim to warn players not to make the pace 'fast and furious'.

The orchestra now warms to the theme, and the woodwind become quite exuberant, with flutes, oboes, and bassoons all trilling to rolling drums. The violin arpeggios busily away, until it reaches a new strenuous, buttress-type theme, an example of Brahms once again contrasting the high jinks of tuneful melodies with some solid construction work by the soloist. This leads to a stormy section, with clouds of brass and shafts of sunlight from the violin, until the repeat of the opening theme is reached.

The violin arpeggios away again absent-mindedly, and then turns up with a completely new tune.

Example 3

p dolce

The orchestra accompanies this digression in a rather bemused way, and, after indulging in the caprice for quite long enough, starts to nag the violin back to the job in hand, by a ponderous insistence on the original rhythm, leading to a massive re-assertion of the main tune. But the violin still wants to 'fiddle away while Rome burns', and goes into a cadenza-like section, with mutters and grumbles from the orchestra saying 'Yes . . . that's all very well. But it's time to be going home. Come on now.' This doesn't work, and the orchestra tries a different tactic. It increases speed, changing the tempo to *poco piú presto* – a little faster – and bassoons, clarinets, and drums, start a march tune with little, rhythmic rolling phrases. The violin is amused, and agrees to go with them. The flutes and oboes are delighted, and seem to burst into peals of laughter. There is a final gallop home, with the violin only pausing to look back in a final *diminuendo* – playing more quietly – at the visionary country it is about to leave.

And so, at the end of the journey, both orchestra and violin have learnt from each other by seeing melodies through the other's eyes. They have argued and contradicted each other, but also shared moments of sublime understanding. The balance has been perfectly kept by Brahms – and Joachim must share the credit too – with the brilliance of the solo part, and the restrained way in which he has used the orchestra; sometimes resting the strings, and giving them a pizzicato (plucking) accompaniment, to allow the violin to achieve its softest moments, and reach the peaks now glimpsed in the distance.

LISTENER'S GUIDE

Piano Concerto no. 2 in B flat, op. 83

This masterly Piano Concerto is a work of Brahms's maturity. A sublime and sometimes playful piece, it reflects the breadth and force of Brahms's vision.

To the young Brahms the piano concerto was a refuge for musical ideas that had gradually evolved as he tried to compose a symphony. Eventually, the First Piano Concerto (1858) was born out of these ideas and out of his desire to impress the world with his virtuosity as a pianist.

The First Piano Concerto is a mighty structure, earnestly symphonic in style and uncompromising in mood, in which the pianist is required to display great virtuosity, though never for its own ends, and the orchestra carries at least an equal weight of the musical argument. Even so, the hard-worked pianist may be forgiven for feeling that his virtuosity is appreciated by the audience not so much for its display of fireworks as for the contribution it makes to the orchestra's final victory.

Deutsche Fotothek Dresden

Brahms (above) began composing his magnificent Second Piano Concerto when he was 45, following his first visit to Italy. The country proved to be a powerful stimulus – he fell in love with the scenery, the people, the architecture and the wonderful intensity of the light (right). He then laid the work aside until a second Italian trip (in 1880) reawakened his interest. The Concerto, completed in 1881, is a passionate and thoughtful work, with some of the graciousness and warmth of his beloved Italy – particularly in the joyous opening to the fourth movement.

Turner 'Ancient Rome; Agrippina landing with the ashes of Germanicus' (detail). The Tate Gallery, London

A mature work

That First Concerto was completed in 1858 when Brahms was 25 years old. He did not return to the form for another 23 years, by which time his idiom had changed and his nature had matured. For Brahms the 48-year-old, the piano concerto was an even broader conception, yet there are concessions to both the listener and the soloist. The musical language is gentler and easier to identify with (though every bit as finely wrought), while the piano part, though still of enormous difficulty, is more sympathetic to the requirements of the instrument. In addition, the demands of classical form are triumphantly satisfied.

Brahms's respect for classical form is here combined with Beethoven's broadening influence and the Romanticism of Schumann in a work of great beauty and considerable difficulty, which even manages to include the odd trace of folk influence. In short, the Piano Concerto no. 2 was, for Brahms, a summing-up of earlier styles.

The first performance

Brahms began studying composition with Eduard Marxsen when he was 16, but he did not neglect his piano playing. His first solo concert took place in 1848 and for many years his career as a composer carried on side-by-side with his career as a concert pianist. He performed his First Piano Concerto in Hanover in 1859 to great applause, but a second performance, in Leipzig, was coldly received. It was not until he had visited Italy in 1878 that he felt emboldened to draft another. Although there is not a trace of Italianate music in the Piano Concerto no. 2, it is not too fanciful to imagine a hint of Mediterranean sunshine in the finale. A second Italian visit reawakened his interest in this draft, which he had neglected while composing his Violin Concerto, and the final touches were put to the Piano Concerto no. 2 in the village of Pressbaum near Vienna, in July 1881. In November Brahms gave its first performance in Budapest.

Corvina Archivum, Budapest

The Second Piano Concerto was premièred in Budapest, in November, 1881, at the premises of the Philharmonic Society (above). Brahms himself was the soloist. Indeed, he thought highly enough of the work to dedicate the published score to his 'dear friend and teacher' Eduard Marxsen (above right). Marxsen, then approaching the end of his life, had taught Brahms many years before.

When composing his Concerto no. 1, Brahms possibly drew upon his experience of Schumann's music, as well as upon Beethoven's (although it is the Beethoven of the Choral Symphony no. 9 in the same key of D minor, rather than the Beethoven of the Emperor Concerto, who glares out through the textures). But he avoided the flashy bravura of Liszt. When he returned to the piano concerto form he had a much richer repertoire to draw upon, had he wished to do so: Grieg and Tchaikovsky, as well as more Liszt and some clever, if slick, music by Saint-Saëns. But Brahms was very much a self-contained composer, any outside influences having to fight their way through a web of intensely critical and heart-searching analysis before being allowed to find a place in the august context of his own music.

Programme notes

Brahms's Piano Concerto no. 2 is often thought of as unique in that, like a symphony, it comprises four movements, one of which is a *scherzo* (a spirited section). The presence of this scherzo movement has puzzled many. Without it, the Concerto would be a perfectly balanced three-movement design, even if the key of B flat were relatively unrelieved; with it, it becomes, some would say, over-long and unwieldy. It is certainly a test of stamina for the soloist who, after an intense and extended first movement, is faced with a second that places an even greater strain on muscles already longing for the comparative respite of a slow movement.

Composers are notoriously misleading when describing their own works. Mozart claimed to have 'completely forgotten' writing his 'Haffner' Symphony; Janáček gave his five-movement work for vast orchestra (including no less than 12 trumpets) less than its due when he called it *Sinfonietta* (Little Symphony); and Vaughan Williams referred condescendingly to each of his works, no matter how extended or complex, as 'tunes'. With Brahms we may detect an uncharacteristic moment of humour in his description of the immensely long Piano Concerto no. 2 with its extraordinary scherzo as 'a teeny-weeny concerto with a teeny-weeny scherzo'. There is no shadow of doubt, however, that he was aware of its greatness and significance, for there was no flippancy in his dedication of it to his 'dear friend and teacher' Eduard Marxsen in acknowledgement of the secure musical training Marxsen had given him, totally without charge, many years before.

First movement – Allegro non troppo

Whether writing symphonies, concertos or any other major work, Brahms could not do otherwise than compose 'symphonically'. Briefly, this means that his thematic material – his melodies – are capable of expansion, evolution, metamorphosis and combination. The music *grows*. Once the melody is grasped, as a whole and in its component parts, it will be encountered countless times in countless different guises throughout the movement. It may pop up in a disguise so complete that it needs a professor to unmask it. Not only is it all part of the enjoyment as old friends reappear in different and surprising contexts, but it provides a beacon of familiarity to light a path through a long

Understanding music:

When Chopin died in 1848 the supremacy of English, French and Viennese piano makers was indisputable. The largest were Broadwoods who employed some 300 workers in their Westminster factory but without using any machinery. Piano-making was a very labour intensive industry: the instruments were fine examples of highly-skilled craftsmanship and were consequently extremely expensive.

Two years later Heinrich Steinway left his native Germany for the United States and in 1853 established in New York the most famous of all piano manufacturers, Steinway and Sons. There already existed a tradition of piano making in America: the cast-iron frame capable of mass production had been patented in 1825.

Steinways were quick to seize upon this important advance in piano design and in 1857 utilized it in their first grand piano, a 'straight strung' instrument in which the strings ran parallel along the length of the frame. Two years later they produced a grand piano which was to set the standard in design right until the present day. This time the strings were stretched across the frame in a fan-like pattern, a technique used previously in the smaller 'square' piano. This 'over-strung' instrument (the bass strings pass diagonally across the treble) permitted the use of longer bass strings which enhanced the tone of the low register.

The cast-iron frame could withstand much greater tension enabling the use of thicker strings, which together with larger hammers to strike them, increased the volume. The rich sonority

and complex stretch of music. Even unrecognized appearances tend to work upon the unconscious to give a feeling of recognition. The ability of a 'symphonist' to produce memorable melodies that submit to this treatment of intense development and change is a measure of his greatness. One such melody is heard at the very beginning on a solo horn:

A simple theme, perhaps, one half answering the other with an almost naive sense of balance. The opening three notes of each half (marked A and D) strike the ear unfailingly at each appearance and prepare it for a new departure, or for a return to base. The triplets (marked B) are a Brahms fingerprint derived from Hungarian folk music, and, again, they strike the ear forcefully each time, even when sounded quietly, because of their contradiction of the basic rhythm. These triplets (B) are the most important device in the movement, as will be heard. The cadences (C, E) – musical endings, like the ends of phrases or sentences – are subtly different from each other: C is expectant, E satisfying.

The Concerto is barely 20 seconds old and already Brahms has introduced a theme imbued with promise, answered with the gentlest of echoes by the piano. He goes on immediately to extend the theme on woodwind, then strings, but the piano breaks in with a dramatic cadenza (a display of virtuosity) that soon introduces the triplet rhythm of B in the right hand in flat contradiction of the left hand's rhythm.

Traces of Hungarian gypsy music in this Concerto, as in many other of Brahms's works, reveal the enduring influence of the Hungarian violinist Eduard Reményi (left), with whom Brahms toured in 1853.

the piano in Brahms's time

of the bass and the bright ringing sound of the high notes was a revelation to contemporary audiences. Here was an instrument capable of filling even the largest concert hall and quite able to compete with the large romantic orchestra. A robust instrument, it was able to survive the punishing demands of the late 19th century virtuosi who attacked the keyboard with tremendous vigour. Tuners and spare pianos, previously a regular feature of concerts, were no longer necessary.

By 1860 all the fundamentals of the modern piano were present. The ability to use longer strings was particularly beneficial to the manufacture of the domestic 'upright' piano, Steinways producing their first 'over-strung' upright in 1863. The 1867 Paris Exhibition fully acknowledged the superiority of what was known as the 'American System'.

German piano makers soon adopted the Steinway as a model, unlike contemporary French and English manufacturers, and by the 1870s Steinways, together with the German firms Blüthner and Bechstein (all founded in 1853), were dominating the platforms of the world as they do today. By the time of Brahms's death in 1897 a piano was in real terms half the price charged by Broadwoods in 1850 and well over half the world's pianos were either German or American.

Brahms (left) was a consummate pianist and his music placed great demands on both the performer and the piano, which developed during his lifetime into the instrument we know today.

Thus, considerable stress is introduced. The full orchestra breaks in, and the theme grows apace, the music being driven irresistibly forward. In due course, the necessary contrast appears as a new melody on violins,

with, however, the triplet rising prominently on the accompanying *pizzicato* (plucked) violas and cellos. This section ends with the opening notes from the first theme – Brahms never forgets nor neglects. A momentary pause, and a new and urgently leaping idea brings a return to the first theme on woodwind and horns, the triplet at first contributed only by the string foundation.

At last it is the piano's turn to examine that first theme, twisting it this way and that as the orchestra joins in to admire its many facets. All at once the horns and bassoons announce a new and shortened version of the second theme, which is developed at length, regardless of the strings' attempts to reintroduce the opening notes of the first theme. In a grand and exciting episode for piano, elements of all three melodies are heard. The exposition closes with an orchestral statement developing the first and second subjects, and the development section itself is brought in by a new version of the horn call, still in the dark key of F minor. This turns to a leaping idea that undergoes much modification as the development progresses, becoming mellower and merging with the first notes of the second theme. In fact, all the material coalesces, so that what began as three distinct ideas becomes one homogeneous sound by the end of the development. It is a miracle of compromise.

Now the recapitulation can begin amid a nebulous rippling piano accompaniment. Brahms continues to mould and develop his material so that, although the same subjects reappear in the same order, every familiar melodic pattern still comes freshly wrapped. The opening horn call, modified but home at last in its original key, announces the long and triumphant coda.

The first movement is so rich and complex that it almost defies analysis. One can listen to it again and again and still discover more of its secrets.

Second movement – Allegro appassionato

This D minor scherzo may have been intended originally for use in the Violin Concerto, but in mood it returns to the angry young Brahms of the Piano Concerto no. 1, also in the same key of D minor.

The piano rushes in impetuously and is answered in sombre tones by lower strings and horns. The character of the music is turbulent, restlessness being accentuated

The Tate Gallery, London

by the disruptive device of a silent downbeat prominently placed in the opening paragraph. This muscular idea stretches its limbs as if preparing for a lengthy run, but a new motif on strings, *piano, tranquillo e dolce* (softly, tranquilly and sweetly), leads the piano into a new vista that turns almost immediately into a more urgent figure that is worth bearing in mind:

The piano extends this figure, along with reminiscences of the opening subject, but eventually returns to the strings' tranquil theme, with an apologetic, 'But you were saying . . .?' All this material is now repeated note for note, and when this point in the movement is reached a second time the tranquil idea is to be heard only in a totally transformed version merged with the first theme.

At full speed the movement collides with the central D major section, slightly slower and with an entirely new bell-like motif on violins. Entirely new? It is in the nature of Brahms's brand of tightly-organized structures that something which sounds new has to be heard with the aural equivalent of lateral thinking, for it is almost certain that it has grown from somewhere. The energetic bell-like figure in this Concerto is none other than the top line of the urgent motif (Example 3) with which the piano digressed earlier, but now altered and expanded into a powerful orchestral statement.

The piano now seems to want to have nothing to do with it, and reacts with a puzzled, withdrawn passage largely in double octaves. The music inhabits a strange world for a space, the piano striking out with an idea that sounds fresh but is actually derived, of course, from earlier material (the lower strings' sombre response to the piano's opening gambit). Briefly, and quietly, the strings play an outline of the bell-like motif, the piano responds with its puzzled double octaves – and the connection between the two clicks into place. In glorious accord the soloist and orchestra celebrate the reconciliation of disparate ideas.

Brahms's lifelong respect for classical forms is well known, and his studies of Haydn may have suggested his next trick: a

The gentle, reflective quality of the third movement, with its rippling piano passages, is mirrored in Sargent's painting of the* Black Brook *(detail, left). The music's emotional power also finds a parallel in Sargent's bold handling of his medium.

false recapitulation. In this device, the music makes as if to restate earlier material, but is diverted by other matters. The piano prematurely suggests the first subject before the orchestra is fully prepared to comply. There is an instant of doubt before the real recapitulation is launched, only to be altered in ways both minor and far-reaching. The conclusion to the movement is completely gripping.

Third movement – Andante

After the strenuous symphonic activity of the first two movements, Brahms sends home his trumpets and drummer and indulges his Romantic soul for our sheer delight. This slow movement is one of Brahms's most sublime creations, and the composer is unselfish enough to give the best tune to an instrument other than the expected piano.

A solo cello sings a heart-warming melody that is then repeated by violins and bassoon; there is also an important oboe contribution. Not until bar 23 does the piano enter to muse discursively upon the cello's theme. The full orchestra firmly brings attention back to the matter in hand, but evidently the soloist sees further, and passionate, possibilities in the melody. These are expounded at length in a bold accompanied cadenza. A return to the opening mood is again suggested, though now with the utmost tact, by violins, and the music works its way through a veiled episode in F sharp major, clarinets adding harmonies above the pianist's figurations, until the cello solo returns. The piano, silent before, embellishes the melody with the gentlest of comments, and the two soloists lay the movement to rest.

Fourth movement – Allegretto grazioso

The first melody is in two parts, each announced by the piano and answered by violins. It is a skipping, joyous creation, reflecting Brahms's visits to the milder clime of Italy, and is taken up by full orchestra (minus trumpets and drums). Notice two massive punctuations by the soloist. The second melody, heralded by the piano's halting reference to the earlier rhythm, has something of Hungary about it. For a moment there is a Slavonic scowl in the woodwind chords, but this is forgotten in the third theme, announced by piano solo, *dolce* (sweetly) and taken up by clarinets over a pizzicato accompaniment. The piano extends this with a new theme, the fourth, and this is picked up by the flute and oboe in octaves before the third melody returns on violins. In the restatement of the 'Hungarian' theme that follows, the piano fills the gaps in the woodwind statement with ringing held chords. Clarinets and pizzicato strings now return with theme three, and this brings a false recapitulation of the first melody (solo oboe), just as in the scherzo. But in this finale there is an extended development section featuring much virtuoso work for the soloist before the way can be cleared for the real recapitulation. When it finally arrives, it is announced by the second part of the first theme, and all the material of which the movement is built is led into new and unexpected directions.

The coda, or tail-piece, brings a slight increase in pace and a completely new way of looking at the first melody. Here, the Italian atmosphere emerges again: the skipping rhythm of that main theme is transformed into a vivid *saltarello* (a lively Italian dance).

The dancing melody of the final movement has all the lightness and brilliance of an Italian dance (below), and more than a touch of Mediterranean sunshine and warmth.

Catel 'Italian Folk dancers'. Neue Pinakothek, Munich/Joachim Blauel/Artothek

Great interpreters

Deutsche Grammophon Productions

The conductor, Eugen Jochum (above).

The pianist, Emil Gilels (above).

Emil Gilels (pianist)
Born in Odessa in 1916, Gilels is heir to the late 19th-century tradition of Russian giants of the keyboard, and there is little doubt that today he stands alongside Sviatoslav Richter in the forefront of living Soviet pianists. This alone shows him to be an artist of the first rank.

After training at Odessa Conservatory he made his first real impact in the 1933 All Union Musicians' Contest, the first of its kind, capturing first prize with a stunning performance. This established him immediately as a performing artist in Russia, though he wisely decided to complete his Odessa studies, graduating in 1935. Pursuing postgraduate studies in Moscow, he nevertheless made his performing débuts outside the Soviet Union in the mid-30s, winning first prize at the 1939 Ysaÿe Festival in Brussels.

Following the war, Gilels was encouraged to pursue his career and broaden it through international appearances, and over the next few years played extensively in both eastern and western Europe. By the mid-50s he was breaking out further afield, and his reputation was soon launched in England and the US, where his outstanding talents were quickly hailed.

Since that time Gilels has steadily progressed in both reputation and performance to the point of being an acknowledged modern master. Honoured in the 1960s with two orders of Lenin, he has often recorded in the West. He has created a significant legacy reflecting the unusually broad range of music which he interprets so outstandingly.

He is a pianist endowed with flawless execution even at extreme speed, and his style is of the vigorous Russian tradition. He also possesses a great degree of sensitivity and has developed an increasing depth of interpretation. Perhaps his most notable recorded performances are his Schubert piano and chamber works, Chopin, Brahms, Beethoven and Bartók.

Eugen Jochum (conductor)
This famous conductor made his successful concert début in 1926 in Munich. He quickly established his reputation in Germany as an opera conductor of great power and resource. By 1934 he was of sufficient national stature to hold the post of musical director at Hamburg Staatsoper, as well as principal conductor of The Hamburg Philharmonic. This post was his until 1949: thus he survived the Nazi years in the same city and with the same orchestra, and was also one of the few conductors who managed to resist or avoid a great deal of the political and cultural pressure of that régime. Evidence of this can be found in the performance of works by such banned composers as Stravinsky, Bartók and Hindemith.

In 1949 Jochum returned to Munich, where he formed the Bavarian Radio Orchestra, which he personally raised to true international standard within a few years. In the post-war period his reputation spread steadily over Europe and the Atlantic as his guest conducting duties multiplied. By 1961, when he began a three-year tenure as co-leader of the Concertgebouw, he was acknowledged as one of the great contemporary conductors, and his career since then has only served to deepen that impression.

Eugen Jochum, though he admits a special affinity for Bruckner, has recorded masterly and authoritative Beethoven symphony cycles, and was awarded the Brahms Medal of the City of Hamburg in recognition of his remarkable understanding of Brahms.

FURTHER LISTENING

Brahms orchestral and instrumental works

Piano concerto no. 1, op. 15 (1858)
In contrast to the Second Piano Concerto, Brahms's earlier essay into this field is from the first bars a dramatic and arresting piece of music. It cost the composer perhaps his longest struggle to get the work completed to his satisfaction, and more than once he almost abandoned a seeming lost cause. The madness and subsequent death of his mentor, Schumann, occurred during its writing, and this deeply affected the tone of the work: an air of tragedy and sad resignation hangs over all three movements. It is from this that the music's real power develops and expands.

Piano pieces, op. 118 (1893)
Years after finishing his last orchestral composition, and quite late in his life, Brahms was still writing some of his most memorable and beautiful works, but in the chamber and solo piano fields. Brahms had always composed from the piano, so it is no surprise to find him returning to it near the end of his life to record some of his most intimate and deeply-felt views and observations. These six piano pieces encompass a whole universe of thought and feeling, and each is a perfectly constructed musical jewel, the like of which very few composers could aspire to.

LISTENER'S GUIDE

Symphony no. 1 in C minor, op. 68

Brahms (above) as an earnest young man. Although he was in his 40s when he wrote his First Symphony, the project had been growing in his mind since he met the Schumanns in 1853.

Brahms embarked on the task of composing his First Symphony with considerable trepidation. Nevertheless, he created a work of great power and intensity.

The long sustained opening to Brahms's First Symphony has an immediate impact on the listener. It is sombre, even funereal – a rare thing in Brahms's work. Six regular timpani strokes fall in each bar of music, while above this measured tread the strings and wind sigh and cry in tortuous lines of comfortless melody. This, clearly, is an introduction to a tense and powerful musical drama.

Brahms completed his First Symphony at the age of 43, in the autumn of 1876. However, it had been begun many years earlier, the long gestation going back perhaps 20 years or more. In 1853, the young composer had visited Robert Schuman and his pianist wife Clara. At that time he had written no orchestral music, but their reaction to the piano pieces that he played was to describe them as 'veiled symphonies'. Clara wrote in her diary that night that the young Brahms would find the true expresion of his genius when he began to write for the orchestra. There can be no doubt that the Schumanns made this view clear to their impressionable young guest.

Brahms was thrilled by Schuntann's unstinting praise. This, in Schumann's fulsome phrases, was 'he that suddenly comes, chosen to express the highest spirit

Joseph Anton Koch 'Schmadribach Falls'. Museum der Bildenden Künste, Leipzig/Robert Harding Picture Library

Brahms's mighty First Symphony conjures up images of the Alpine scenery that he loved, and which directly inspired the Alpine melody of the Symphony's finale. The work as a whole suggests two contrasting landscapes. The emotional force of the first and last movements, with their fierce and concentrated music, suggests a dark, stormy and dramatic landscape (left). Yet, in the middle movements, which almost serve as graceful interludes, the sun seems to break through the clouds, shedding light on a leisurely and tranquil scene (right).

of the times'. The language (maybe as Schumann intended) unmistakably suggests a John the Baptist announcing a Messiah. But if Brahms did regard himself as a man with a mission, he nevertheless remained a clear-headed and even cautious northener. And, highly self-critical as he was, he knew his limitations. Could he ever write the great symphony that was expected of him?

We know that he tried. Between 1854 and 1859 he drafted out at least part of a symphony. Significantly, he wrote his ideas down in a two-piano form: it seems that he found it hard to escape from thinking in keyboard terms, since, when this symphony was abandoned, many of its ideas were used in his First Piano Concerto. This concerto is a turbulent piece, and it seems that the abandoned symphony must have been a dark and stormy work. Doubtless it reflected the composer's involuntary participation in the tragic events (suicide attempt, madness, death) that overtook Schumann only months after their meeting.

It is probable that the idea of writing a symphony became permanently associated in Brahms's mind with Schumann: such a work, if and when he eventually came to write it, would be intended as both a fulfilment of the older man's generous prophecy and a tribute to him. Certainly he went on thinking about composing a symphony. He was willing to exchange his thoughts on the subject with Clara Schumann, with whom he maintained a lifelong friendship, and she in turn was quite happy to prompt him gently. On 21 June, 1860 she wrote in a letter to Brahms:

Men like yourself respond to the charms of Nature and so nourish the soul. This I gather from the description in your letter. Such a sky of storms may lead to a symphony.

Two years later, she was to see the beginning of her reward. She wrote to a mutual friend of theirs, the violinist Joseph Joachim: 'What do you think Johannes sent me recently? The first movement of a symphony which begins like this . . .

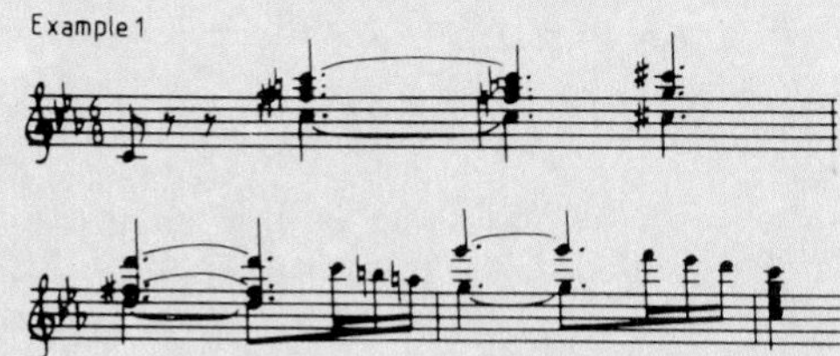

'This *is* rather severe, but I've got used to it. The movement is full of beauties and the themes are treated with a mastery which is more and more individual. The interweaving of material is most interesting, the music flows on and the listener doesn't notice the workmanship . . .'

However, Clara Schumann was, as it turned out, rather premature when she told Brahms that Joachim hoped to conduct his new symphony during the winter of 1862–3. There was no sign of the composer finishing the work in time. In November, 1863, Clara enquired again from Brahms as to its progress, but received no answer. Within the next couple of years the conductor Hermann Levi tried his luck, more than once: 'Why do you persist in your silence? What about that C minor Symphony?' Another conductor, Albert Dietrich, begged Brahms for the work in 1866, but it remained unfinished. A fellow-composer, Max Bruch, wrote to Brahms still later, on 6 May, 1870, 'You really should make up your mind and complete the sketches of your symphony'.

We may wonder what was going on in Brahms's mind during these years. There was no question of a creative block, for he was writing music all this time. But this was not orchestral music, of which he composed none whatsoever during the 1860s. Brahms seems to have convinced himself that it was with nothing less than a masterpiece that he should make his début as a symphonist. And he seems at times to have had doubts as to his powers. In 1870, he actually told Hermann Levi, 'I'll never get a symphony written. You've no conception of what it's like to hear a giant's footsteps marching behind you.'

The giant was evidently the formidable figure of Beethoven. Brahms had already been called 'Beethoven's heir' in Vienna by performers of his chamber works and he knew very well that his First Symphony would be expected to be a worthy successor to Beethoven's Ninth – a new masterpiece composed, if not exactly in the same style, at least in the same tradition. (He was right, and the new symphony, when it finally appeared, was to be hailed as 'Beethoven's Tenth'.)

Friedrich Zimmermann 'Lake of the Engstlen Alp'. Victoria & Albert Museum

But whatever his doubts and difficulties, little by little Brahms was approaching his goal. By 1868, he had already sent Clara Schumann the famous solo horn melody from the symphony's finale as a kind of alpine tune, to the words 'High on the mountain, deep in the valley, I greet you many thousand times.'

And now, too, Brahms was perfecting his orchestral technique. In 1868 he had finished his *German Requiem* with its orchestral-choral texture, and his increasing experience as a conductor earned him the directorship of the Vienna Philharmonic Orchestra. By conducting his own and other composers' music he gained the kind of inside knowledge of the orchestra that he needed for real instrumental mastery. In 1873, he produced his 'St Anthony' Variations for orchestra, and the Vienna Philharmonic Orchestra gave their première under the conductor Otto Dessoff on 2 November. The audience and press reaction was favourable, and once again raised the question of why this very gifted composer, now 40, had not yet offered the public a symphony. 'After this incomparable feat', wrote one admirer, 'your followers will look forward all the more eagerly to the long-awaited symphony.'

Indeed, Brahms was now on the last lap of this most taxing of his creative journeys. At last he was able to promise the work to his publisher Simrock, and finally, in September, 1876, he completed the symphony. He played it to Clara Schumann a month later – who felt it lacked melody, but reserved judgement until she heard it 'properly on the orchestra'. (Later she changed her mind and became a warm admirer of the work.) At the last minute Brahms shortened the two middle movements. Finally the Symphony was ready for performance. The première took place under Otto Dessoff at Karlsruhe, on 4 November, 1876.

Brahms had spent 20 years and more composing this masterpiece. Evidently he followed his own advice about composition: writing to a fellow-composer in 1876, the year of the Symphony's completion, he urged,

Go over it again and again until there's not a bar you can improve on . . . I never go 'off the boil' with a work once I've started it until it is unassailably perfect.

Critical reactions to the First Symphony

Within a few weeks of the First Symphony's first performance in November 1876, the composer himself conducted performances in Mannheim, Munich, Vienna, Leipzig and Breslau. It was also performed on March 8, 1877 in England, where Joachim conducted the Cambridge University Musical Society.

Most opinions of the new work were favourable. It formed, said the English composer Sir Charles Stanford, 'an imperishable keystone to Brahms's fame among Britons'. For the Viennese critic Hanslick, the symphony made clear 'Brahms's close affinity with Beethoven . . . [it] displays an energy of will, a logic of musical thought, a greatness of structural power and a mastery of technique such as are possessed by no other living composer'. A Leipzig musician wrote that 'its effect on the audience was the most intense that has been produced by any new symphony within memory . . . the composition is to be measured from the standpoint of Beethoven's Ninth.' Several commentators referred to the darker side of the work: one went so far as to write that in the introduction of the first movement and again in the finale, 'the enigmatical Sphinx seems to call to us'. Several people noted the resemblance between the big theme of the finale and that in the finale of Beethoven's Ninth Symphony. A resemblance can indeed be traced and was perhaps deliberate, but the general effect is totally different – and highly original.

Clara Schumann remained a loyal but honest critic. Speaking as one who had known Brahms's music almost from the first, she expressed, along with her praise, a few reservations: 'The end of the third movement did not quite satisfy me – it's too short.' And she found the *coda* to the finale slightly unconvincing: 'it appears added on as a brilliant finish.' One can perhaps see what Clara meant, but few people today would agree with her as regards the end of the symphony. Was it simply that, knowing Brahms personally, she recognized that the tragic elements in the work were closer to the 'real' Brahms than the exuberant joy of its final moments? Whatever the truth, the triumphant *coda* now seems a fitting end to this grand symphony.

Programme notes

Brahms's First Symphony is in the usual four movements. The first is an *Allegro,* preceded by a slower introduction. Then comes the slow movement, marked *Andante sostenuto.* Instead of the conventional brisk 'scherzo' third movement, Brahms then gives us a sort of leisurely dance, *Un poco allegretto e grazioso.* The finale, like the first movement, starts with a slow introduction, which gradually reaches a main tempo of *Allegro non troppo ma con brio* – in other words a speed that is fairly (but not excessively) brisk, yet vigorous. The last few pages (the vivid closing section which is called a *coda*) are *Più Allegro,* (faster).

First movement: Un poco sostenuto – Allegro

Over heavy drum (timpani) beats, six to a bar in two groups of three, the strings and wind wail a disquieting lament. Brahms marks it *forte* (loud) but also 'expressive', in other words designed to convey emotional force. This first, and quite alarming statement is answered by a softer one: angular, offbeat phrases for the woodwind instruments (flutes, oboes, clarinets, bassoons) which are doubled by *pizzicato* (plucked) strings. A curious rocking pattern of notes on the strings, once again played normally with the bow, is the next thing to engage our attention: it rapidly builds up to an even more anguished statement of the opening music.

There is clearly much purpose in what

Brahms thought naturally in terms of the piano (right). The first ideas for this Symphony were in two-piano form, and were later used in the First Piano Concerto.

Clara (above), the wife of Brahms's friend and champion, Robert Schumann, both inspired and prompted Brahms to write the First Symphony.

The stressful opening of the First Symphony seems to reflect Brahms's love for Clara. Of a melancholy work composed at the same time, Brahms wrote: 'You might put a portrait on the title page! A head with a pistol in front of it . . . I will send you my photograph! Can you also have a blue dress-coat, yellow pantaloons and top boots . . .? The reference was to Goethe's hero Werther (above), who shot himself because he was in love with his best friend's wife.

we have just heard. In fact, the three themes or motifs – the wailing rising string figure, the angular woodwind phrases, the rocking figure too – are all to reappear as principal themes of the *Allegro* which is to follow and for which this introduction is preparing us. In the meantime a plaintive solo oboe seems to clear the gathering storm clouds of the opening away.

Now the *Allegro*, at its brisk pace, bursts out very loudly *(fortissimo)* with the principal theme. This is built up from the rising notes (which introduce it) and the rocking figure, played respectively by the wind instruments and the strings. Then the strings, in a massive unison statement, answer with the angular, falling motif that we previously heard in the introduction played quietly by the woodwind and *pizzicato* strings. Brahms is at his most powerful and concentrated here, advancing the music with brisk stern strides, and actually marking it to be played 'heavily' *(pesante)*. Loudness, with brief respites, is the order of the day, and the rocking figure seems to drive the music forwards with its long-short loping rhythm, sometimes heard smoothly (*legato* is the technical term) and sometimes detached *(staccato)*.

Gradually the music calms itself, diminishing in loudness though maintaining the brisk and purposeful *Allegro* speed. Brahms has now changed key from the main tonality (key) of C minor to the different though closely related E flat major: this is normal symphonic procedure, as it is here that the second principal theme or subject of the movement is to be introduced. But what is unusual about this particular second subject – played by the oboe and answered by the strings – is that it is really nothing more than a variant of the first theme that opened the *Allegro,*

By 1868, Brahms had sent Clara the famous horn melody from the Symphony's finale set to the words 'High on the mountain, deep in the valley, I greet you many thousand times' (below). It was intended as a birthday gift, and no doubt as a tribute to Clara.

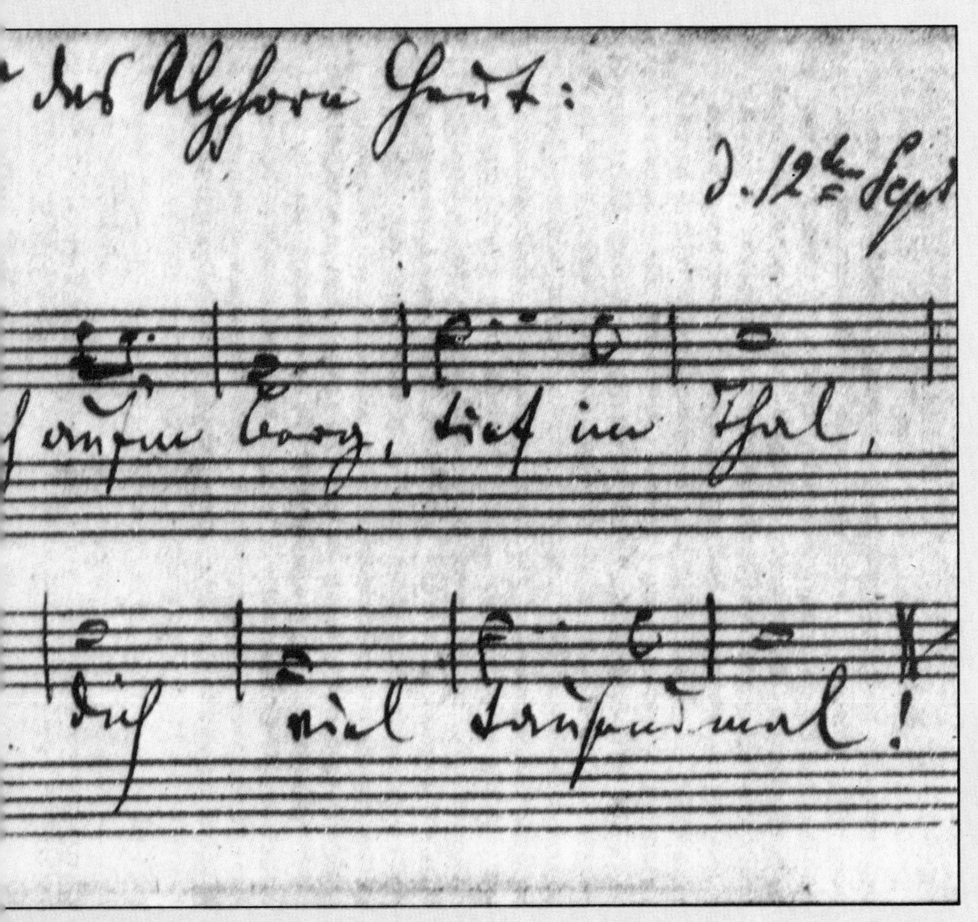

which was in its turn derived from the material of the introduction. However, played like this, expressively as Brahms marks it to be and now in the major instead of the minor mode, it does sound like a new tune in a new, darkening mood. This second theme has an extra motif which gives it a particular character of its own.

This is the point in the first movement where, conventionally, we approach the end of the exposition, but Brahms still has another stormy theme to present to us. Its main feature is three rapid descending notes, and it bursts in with an urgent crescendo on the strings.

This three-note figure is hardly new, though until now we have heard it smoothly rising rather than descending.

Österreichische Nationalbibliothek, Vienna © Willi von Beckerath

Abrupt two-note figures like an angry cuckoo-call mark the end of the opening section. Sometimes the whole of the exposition is repeated, but this depends on the conductor: some, like Karajan, with the Vienna Philharmonic Orchestra, carry straight on into the development.

The composer now takes us into new keys – B major is the first of them – and to a new and more mysterious, expressive atmosphere, in which the themes we already know seem to creep about in greater or lesser disguise. Now our thir theme (Example 4) breaks in forcefully but only to lead on to a new idea, smoot and grand:

This is one of the few optimistic moment in the first movement and perhaps for thi

Understanding music: the role of the conductor

Nowadays, the conductor is a familiar figure to concert-goers. The imposing stance and commanding position seem an integral part of any performance of a symphony. Indeed, the charisma of conductors like Karajan is such that performances are rated by their role as much as by the quality of the orchestra. Yet it was not always so.

As music has changed over the ages, so has the need for direction. At its simplest, the conductor's role is simply to beat time. When music was fairly primitive, there was no need for time keeping to be assigned to one person – in Ancient Greece, the rhythm of a piece was maintained by stamping on the ground; and clapping has been quite adequate for hundreds of years.

But as music became more formalized and more complex so the need for some sort of direction grew. In the chants of medieval churches, even though the 'tunes' were simple, it was important that the voices should all rise and fall together. So the choir had a *director,* whose badge of office was a staff. But the staff was only for show; he directed the choir with his free left hand.

Yet for the complex music of the 16th and 17th century, even this was not precise enough. The band needed someone to beat time very accurately. At first directors would mark time with their staff of office, but this staff, often many feet long, was too cumbersome for the fast, complex music that was growing in popularity. Some directors used a smaller stick – some simply used a roll of paper, which could be seen easily even in dimly lit rooms.

In opera, the complexity of directing both a large cast of singers moving around on stage and a fairly sizeable orchestra called for a different solution. Often there would be two directors – the keyboard player who would provide the accompaniment for the singers; and the principal violinist who would direct the orchestra. This practice was adopted for concerts and recitals and in the late 18th and early 19th century, composers such as Mozart would often sit at the keyboard directing their latest piece – a position where they could exert maximum control, since the keyboard often laid down the rhythmic basis for the whole piece (the *continuo*).

As the need for a keyboard continuo disappeared, so the idea of a director at the keyboard seemed increasingly redundant. At first, the principal violinist would take over, but soon the growing size of the orchestra and the increasing complexity of orchestral arrangements made this impractical too. Soon the familiar figure of the conductor standing in front of the orchestra, visible to all the musicians, directing with a little stick or 'baton' began to be more and more commonplace.

Composers, who had a keen interest in seeing their music properly played, did a great deal to establish the prominence of the conductor. Weber and Spohr both played a significant role, but it was Wagner and Berlioz who had the most dramatic effect. Wagner emphasized the conductor's role in choosing the tempo of the piece; Berlioz stressed the psychological problems. Both composers also wrote significant treatises on conducting.

During the latter half of the 19th century, the role of the conductor began to assume more and more significance – perhaps as 'interpretation' became more important – and musicians who specialized in conducting alone emerged. Indeed, conducting gradually became one of the highest callings of the performing musician.

These lively pencil sketches, by an eye-witness, show Brahms conducting one of his own works with typical breadth and composure (left). The First Symphony was itself conducted by Brahms, in Mannheim, Munich, Vienna, Leipzig and Breslau. These performances took place within a few weeks of the Symphony's première in November, 1876.

reason it is unusually effective. Quiet and forceful musical sequences alternate in this dramatic development.

After that, we are once again on familiar ground: here the recapitulation (restatement section) starts with the same music, essentially, as the beginning of the *Allegro.* The second theme is still played by the oboe, but this time in the movement's main key of C, which at this point is major rather than minor. At the end of this restatement section, which is both regular and easy to follow, we move into the *coda* or closing section that derives largely from what has been irreverently called the two-note cuckoo-call figure. Finally, the speed slackens for a last reminder of the first theme and a soft, subdued close that is somehow inconclusive: Brahms's drama is not yet over.

Second movement: Andante sostenuto

The second movement is a much more relaxed piece. It is in E major, and in this rather remote key it seems to speak of a deep calm, perhaps some nocturnal Alpine scene that Brahms enjoyed on a Swiss or Austrian holiday: the gentle sound of the two horns helps us to imagine this. A tune played by the violins gently unfolds, to be answered by the solo oboe. These two instrumental colours – violins and oboe – alternate, and gradually the mood becomes more animated and the instrumentation more florid. The opening melody returns richly on woodwind: note the *pizzicato* (plucked) cellos here as well as the first use in this movement of timpani and trumpets. The 'answer' that was originally played by the oboe is now given, somewhat romantically, to the solo violin, which dominates the rest of the movement almost as in a *concerto* (a composition for a solo instrument accompanied by the orchestra). A gentle coda, crowned by a poignant violin solo, ends the piece.

Third movement: Un poco allegretto e grazioso

The third movement of Brahms's First Symphony is marked *Un poco allegretto e grazioso,* implying a leisurely yet gracefully-moving tempo. The clarinet at once gives us a main theme, effortlessly floating along in the warm key of A flat major, while a kind of dance element is provided by the bass line of plucked cellos. If the *andante* second movement seemed to speak of a nocturnal landscape, this third

Like many composers in the late 18th century, Haydn would often direct his music from the keyboard. This practice originated in opera, where the director would play the accompaniment while directing the singers on stage.

Beethoven-Haus, Bonn

Brahms was considered to be the natural heir to Beethoven (above). His First Symphony was immediately hailed as 'Beethoven's Tenth'.

movement suggests radiant sunlit countryside. Brahms's own frequent marking of *dolce* (sweetly, gently) here appears almost unneccessary, since the notes seem already bathed in a warm contented glow. Descending scales in a long-short ('dotted') rhythm introduced new fragments of melody over a quietly bouncing string accompaniment, but the first real new theme comes with the central section. This involves a change of key, to B major, and its beginning is unmistakable, with three-note figures alternating between the wind instruments and the strings. The mood becomes distinctly boisterous, but remains carefree. After that, the original clarinet theme of the opening inevitably returns, though Brahms retains our full interest by combining it with the middle-section tune and taking it into further leisurely adventures before the calm yet still playful ending.

Fourth movement: Allegro non troppo ma con brio

It is easy to forget at this point that we have been listening to a 'tragic symphony' – for so Brahms's First has been called. Occasionally people have wondered whether the two middle movements are a little light for the mighty first movement and finale. In any case, Brahms now reminds us that we are listening to a highly dramatic work. The Finale begins, like the first movement, with a strident cry of pain. Later on these first six notes, played by the violins in a tense high register, will be transformed into one of the most buoyant and cheering melodies of the symphonic repertory, worthy to stand beside the great tune in Beethoven's Ninth Symphony with which it has always been compared.

But let's not anticipate. This introduction to the finale is troubled and searching. There are curious *pizzicato* passages that suggest groping about in darkness, anxiously if not quite hopelessly. And then, as Sir Donald Tovey put it, 'day breaks. There is no more tragedy'. A horn solo marked 'passionately', rings out like the Alpine horn call that inspired it; the key is a splendidly affirmative C major; the hymn-like chords played by trombones and bassoons only deepen the healing mood. Now the main part of the finale follows on from the dramatic introduction. The 'big tune', in C major, of a jubilant march-like, character, is one of those rare melodies which, once heard, can really never be forgotten. It is repeated by the flutes and then *(animato)* is developed with giant strides. A new melody appears now: this is quieter, in the new key of G major, and marked both *animato* and *dolce* (gently):

From here onwards Brahms seems quite uninhibitedly to let his imagination have free rein. What sounds like a new theme, with his favourite long-short, long-short rhythm, is however derived from the introduction. After much exuberance and energy, the big tune returns, marked *largamente* (broadly).

And now we are approaching the end of the finale, and of Brahms's whole mighty symphony. The 'Alpine' horn solo returns, introduced (something of a master-stroke, this) by a jagged and rapid high-strings version of itself. Now it is the turn of the second melody (Example 6) to reappear, a little later than we expected it, once again *dolce, animato* – gentle but nonetheless lively – and in the home key of C major for what is now the 'home straight' of the symphony. The music is once again familiar. But then it moves via a brief, quiet passage into the brilliant *coda.*

This concluding section is marked *Più Allegro,* (faster), and has a repeated three-note figure that is identical with the first three notes of the 'big tune'. The jubilant mood is briefly interrupted, or perhaps enhanced, by a reference to the hymn-like chords that we have heard only once before, in the introduction. The end, without any slackening of pace, is colossally affirmative, as affirmative as that of Beethoven's Fifth Symphony, which – and could it possibly be coincidence, knowing Brahms's reverence for the older master? – is in the same key, C minor becoming C major.

Great interpreters

Herbert von Karajan (conductor)

Herbert von Karajan, the famous Austrian conductor, was born in Salzburg in 1908. He began his musical career by studying the piano, before changing direction and studying conducting under Franz Schalk at the Vienna Academy.

His first public success came when he conducted Mozart's *Marriage of Figaro* in March 1929 at Ulm, where he remained for five years working at the Städtisches Theater. It was here that he developed an emphasis on strict discipline and a taste for firmness and cleanness of line in both conducting and producing. In 1934, he was appointed *Generalmusikdirektor* at Aachen, and in 1937 consolidated his success in a memorable performance of Wagner's *Tristan und Isolde* in Berlin. From 1941, he made Berlin his home.

After the Second World War, Karajan, like many Berliners, found the peace disrupted rather than helped his career. However, in 1947 he returned to the limelight with a series of concerts with the Vienna Symphony Orchestra and a legendary recording of Richard Strauss's *Metamorphosen* with the Vienna Philharmonic. This interpretation was looked upon at the

time as a requiem for a shattered Germany, and was one of the seminal events in establishing Karajan's international reputation. In the same year, Karajan also made his successful London début.

From 1948–9, Karajan combined the roles of conductor and opera producer at La Scala, Milan, while also embarking on an extensive recording programme with the London Philharmonic. He made his American début in 1955 with the Berlin Philharmonic – the orchestra with which his name was now almost synonymous.

In 1956 he was made artistic director of the Salzburg festival (until 1960) and in 1957, succeeded Karl Böhm as director of the Vienna Staatsoper. Following artistic disagreements, he resigned his Vienna post in 1964 (returning in 1977) and again took up his post at the Salzburg festival. His interest in therapy and conducting technique, prompted him to set up the Herbert von Karajan Foundation in 1969, which stages competitions from promising young conductors and organizes scientific conferences on a wide variety of different subjects.

Deutsche Grammophon Production

The Vienna Philharmonic (right), one of the finest orchestras in the world, performing in the magnificent surroundings of the Musikvereinsaal in Vienna. The charismatic conductor, Herbert von Karajan (below), is absorbed in the music.

Deutsche Grammophon Production

Karajan's performances were highly electric and emotional, combining a concern for technical precision with a love of lush and dense orchestral texture and colouring. His fierce dynamism and sensuous approach to instrumentation made him one of the most romantically-minded conductors. A renowned interpreter of Mozart operas, perhaps his most distinguished achievement in orchestral music was in the Beethoven, Brahms and Mahler symphonic cycles. Herbert von Karajan died in 1989.

The interpretation

Karajan's interpretation of Brahm's First Symphony is powerful, almost Olympian. He takes a particularly weighty approach to the first movement, evincing a stormy and tragic view of the music. With the middle movements, he takes a relatively light approach, treating the music almost as if it were a sunny interlude. But the dynamism returns with the last movement which is strident and jubilant. The warmth and colour of the music is emphasized by the rich tone of the Vienna Philharmonic's string section which is perhaps the finest in the world.

FURTHER LISTENING

Brahms orchestral works

Variations on a theme by Haydn, op. 56a
Often regarded as Brahms's first completely successful orchestral piece, the Haydn Variations demonstrate the composer's overriding concern with strict control over his musical materials. They show his approach to be that of a man obsessed with 'absolute' music – music which tells no stories and illustrates no themes or ideas, and which remains wholly self-sufficient.

Symphony no. 4 in E minor, op. 98
Brahms's last symphony, and his penultimate orchestral work, is generally regarded as one of the world's great symphonic masterpieces. It combines rigorous control of the structure with great daring in the choice of classical forms. A towering and majestic work, it nevertheless exhibits great warmth and expansiveness in its slower movements.

Alto Rhapsody, op. 53
Some of Brahms's most sublime musical achievements were made in his choral writing. This relatively short piece for alto singer, chorus and orchestra is a setting of a fragment from Goethe's *Sorrows of Young Werther*. For all its brevity, its impact, achieved through the inspired shift from a sombre opening to the chorale-like ending, is deep and lasting.

Great interpreters

The conductor: Bernard Haitink

The violinist: Henryk Szeryng.

Bernard Haitink (conductor)

Born in Amsterdam in 1929, Haitink first took lessons on the violin as a child. After training at the Amsterdam Conservatory, he joined the Netherlands Radio Philharmonic on violin. In 1954 and '55, while still in his early 20s, he took courses in conducting which had been organized by the Netherlands Radio Union. Here he was recognised as an emerging talent and guided by the great Ferdinand Leitner. At the end of these courses he was appointed second conductor for the Radio Union: his duties included the directing of four different radio orchestras. By 1957 he had secured the position of principal conductor with the Netherlands Radio Philharmonic.

His association with the world-famous Concertgebouw commenced through a last-minute hiring as a guest conductor for a Cherubini concert in 1956. The success of his unscheduled début led to regular guest appearances over the next few years and, with the death of Eduard van Beinum in 1961, to his appointment as joint principal conductor with Eugen Jochum. He was the orchestra's youngest-ever incumbent. With Jochum's departure in 1964, Haitink assumed sole responsibility.

As his reputation spread abroad, he began an association with the London Philharmonic Orchestra which was to blossom into his becoming, from 1967 to 1979, its principal conductor and artistic advisor. During this period he divided his time equally between these two orchestras, building up an enviable reputation in the music world. By the early 70s he was ready to branch out into opera, and he has been a regular guest at Glyndebourne and, since 1977, Covent Garden.

Haitink today enjoys the high esteem of both critics and fellow-musicians, and is undoubtedly in the forefront of modern conductors. In the orchestral music field his sensitive, thoroughly-researched and deeply felt conducting of Mahler and Bruckner cycles are models of their kind. At present he is nearing completion of a recording project involving the complete Shostakovich symphony cycle, and the performances so far released indicate it to be a towering achievement.

Haitink established his conducting career with the late romantics such as Mahler and Bruckner, Tchaikovsky and Brahms, but has since become a committed interpreter of an impressively broad spectrum of music stretching back to Haydn and Mozart and forward to present-day Dutch composers such as Otto Ketting. A brilliant and incisive musical analyst, his keen intelligence and artistic conviction bring immense authority to everything he conducts.

Henryk Szeryng (violinist)

Polish-born, Szeryng studied the piano as a child, but soon switched to the violin, the instrument which was to win him world-wide fame. In 1928, at the age of 10, he was sent to study in Berlin, and he progressed rapidly, making his performing début in 1933 in a variety of cities. His studies continued apace and, in the six years between 1933 and 1939, he studied composition under the redoubtable Nadia Boulanger in Paris.

With the advent of the Second World War, Szeryng's fluency in many languages brought him to the attention of the Polish government-in-exile, and he was duly appointed to the diplomatic staff. In this capacity he travelled throughout the world publicizing the plight of Polish refugees. Coupled with this were further musical exploits, and he became an indefatigable concert-giver for allied troops in every arena of the war, from Europe and Asia to the Americas. By the end of the war he had given more than 300 performances.

During this period he had visited Mexico on state business and was immediately attracted to it. In the aftermath of the war in Europe he decided to emigrate to Mexico, and in 1946 he took up a teaching position at the National University. Finally, he adopted Mexican citizenship and nationality.

After a hiatus of close to eight years, he resumed international concert touring in 1954, mainly through the encouragement of his friend, the great concert pianist Arthur Rubinstein. Within a very few years his extensive touring had established him as a commanding figure on his instrument, embodying such pre-war values as cleanness of execution, clarity of tone and a superlative elegance of styling. With both technical and stylistic virtuosity assured, his repertoire was a very broad one, though the natural qualities of his style gave most authority to his playing of Mozart and the great romantic concertos, especially those of Beethoven and Brahms.

Szeryng has remained a citizen of Mexico, doing much to promote the often underrated works of that country's composers. He has in recent years divided his time between his teaching commitments in his adopted home and teaching of selected students overseas, combined with a carefully chosen concert itinerary.

FURTHER LISTENING

Brahms's orchestral and chamber works

Double Concerto, op. 102
This Concerto is the very last of Brahms's works for orchestra. The unusual combination of violin and cello as dual soloists probably came as a result of their prominence in the chamber works written immediately before it. It certainly led to this Concerto being far-ranging in ideas and expression through the extraordinary writing for the two lead instruments, whether playing alone or in unison, with the orchestra's support or without it. A profusion of arresting themes and ingenious variations showcase the typical combination of intellect and emotion which is a highlight of Brahms at his best.

Academic Festival Overture, op. 80
In 1879 Brahms was awarded a doctorate from Breslau University. This gave him an opportunity to indulge himself with a small concert piece in a light vein as a recognition of the honour. Though by nature a serious man, Brahms here showed himself to be perfectly capable of turning out a wholly enjoyable, light-hearted score, with a spirited working of popular and folk material.

Clarinet Quintet in B minor, op. 115
The Quintet is quite simply one of the most beautiful pieces of music Brahms ever wrote, and is certainly his loveliest chamber work. Written towards the end of his life, it is full of autumnal warmth and tenderness. The elegaic Adagio, in particular, shows the surety of touch in combining the clarinet's pure, elusive tone with the sonority of the strings. Brahms's heart is, for once, clearly on his sleeve.

In the background

Scientists still argue about which contributes most to our personalities, talents and behaviour: the inheritance of our genes or the influence of our environment. However, it is undeniable that we cannot help but be affected to some extent by our surroundings, both in the narrow sense of our personal backgrounds and in the wider sense of the times in which we live. Great composers are no exception, and the following pages describe the historical background to Brahms's life and the political, economic and cultural events that influenced and inspired him: the economic and social upheavals in Germany that drove many people to escape their desperate situation by emigrating to the United States; the career of Prince Otto von Bismarck, the Iron Chancellor, whose warlike policy united the small states of Germany into an empire headed by the royal house of Prussia; and the development of middle-class tourism in 19th-century Europe.

IN THE BACKGROUND

Destination America

Most people, especially those who own or who live off the land, are greatly attached to their home country, and they have to be highly motivated before they can think of leaving permanently. Conditions in Germany in the 19th century provided such stimuli for many people. Emigrants wanted to escape economic problems caused by crop failure and cheap imports; they wanted to find a society where there were no kings or oppressive governments and where there was plenty of land for those willing to work hard. Such a place was the United States, and during Brahms's life-time hundreds of thousands of Germans joined other nationalities who were hoping to start afresh in the New World. Many Germans did make good, and gave their names – such as Faber, Steinweg (Steinway) and Pabst – to some of America's most famous manufacturing companies.

IN THE BACKGROUND

'Yearning to be free'

Hamburg, where Brahms grew up, was an important exit port for German emigrants – men and women who crossed the Atlantic in the hope of a better life in the New World.

An emigrant family's last sight of home (above). America was the Mecca for thousands of such families in the 19th century.

1816 was a very strange year. The summer never came. Hot weather and humid rains in February gave way to intense cold in April, and in May the wells in many German farms froze solid. June brought thunderstorms and hail which continued until September. Old people and children alike died from hunger and from cold. An extraordinary plague of mice invaded fields and villages in many areas. Finally, in October, the wretched harvest began, but before it could be completed the fields were covered in snow. Peasants hacked through the ice for frozen potatoes. People ate anything they could. A professor of medicine in Tübingen published a booklet entitled, 'A Thorough Introduction to the Preparation of Bread out of Wood'.

The freakish weather and pathetic harvest were all the more catastrophic because in 1816 German farmers were eagerly awaiting the first fruits of peacetime after the havoc of the Napoleonic wars. They had suffered enough disruption when their crops had been taken by the armies and by the state, and now they were hoping that everything would return to normal. But instead, during that fateful year, things got worse. The sudden disappearance of the military markets convulsed the economy, while the flood of cheap manufactured goods from Britain to the Continent also had a disastrous effect on the livelihood of local craftsmen. After the bitterly disappointing harvest of 1816, people began to think of another way out of their misery – and for the most

Für westliche Einwanderer!
Iowa Land
im Thale des
Des Moines Flusses.
Minnesota
Wisconsin
L. MICHIGAN
Nebraska
Kansas
Missouri
Eine Million A
Zu verkaufen gegen Credit von der
Des Moines Navigation Com
354 From a broadside (no date) of the Des Moines N

Peter Newark's Western Americana

Some American companies made great efforts to attract European immigrants, and they concentrated their publicity (left) on relatively affluent areas such as Germany. Single men usually left depressed rural communities (right) first, and their kin followed. But there were cases of whole villages emigrating together.

Starving peasants search for potatoes (right). Life on the land held no sentimental value for people driven abroad by famine, and they generally settled in cities.

BBC Hulton Picture Library

Leon Lhermitte 'La Paye des Moissonneurs'. Lauros-Giraudon © DACS 1987

daring and enterprising folk emigration seemed like a possible answer.

The fever of 1816

By the end of 1816 the first large-scale example of *Auswanderung* (emigration) was under way in southern and western Germany. In the Duchy of Württemburg officials issued passports for 18,000 travellers – two per cent of the population was leaving. The old order had fallen apart politically; artisans could find no markets for their goods; and now the peasants and farmers had seen their work destroyed by an act of God. For thousands of poor people this was the final proof that they had no reason to remain. As this small but unprecedented stream of travellers passed through Germany, they spread the idea that people could end their misfortune by emigrating. Like a virus, the idea did not catch on immediately but lay dormant until triggered by some local circumstance in the towns and communities they passed through.

In response to the phenomenon, a German newspaper commented:

In the richest and fairest parts of Europe there rules such discontent that whole families resolve to quit their fatherland. The spirit of restlessness and dissatisfaction is so general and so widespread that it must have a more profound cause than human foolishness. We are bound by the eternal bonds of

Nature to the ground upon which life welcomed us and we enjoyed our happiest years, where parents, kinsmen, and so many departed friends rest; and only a power stronger than all those attachments can break so strong a bond. He must be truly unfortunate who will give up a certain present for a doubtful future, his homeland for an alien country, the known for the unknown.

These pioneering travellers were heading for the farthest frontiers they had heard of: North America and Asiatic Russia (which did not endure as a favoured destination). Those hoping to cross the Atlantic travelled down the Rhine to the ports of the Netherlands, which were soon overcrowded with destitute emigrants who could only reach America by selling themselves as contract labourers to the ships' captains.

Soon, however, the Netherlands authorities became so alarmed by penniless travellers overcrowding the ports that they closed the border to emigrants. The harvest of 1817 was good, and this, combined with stories of sick and disappointed travellers returning from miserable experiences was sufficient to stem the emigration fever. The *Auswanderung* of 1816 was limited but intense. It quickly abated, and a reaction against emigration persisted through the 1820s. But it had inaugurated a pattern which was to be resurrected whenever the economy grew worse.

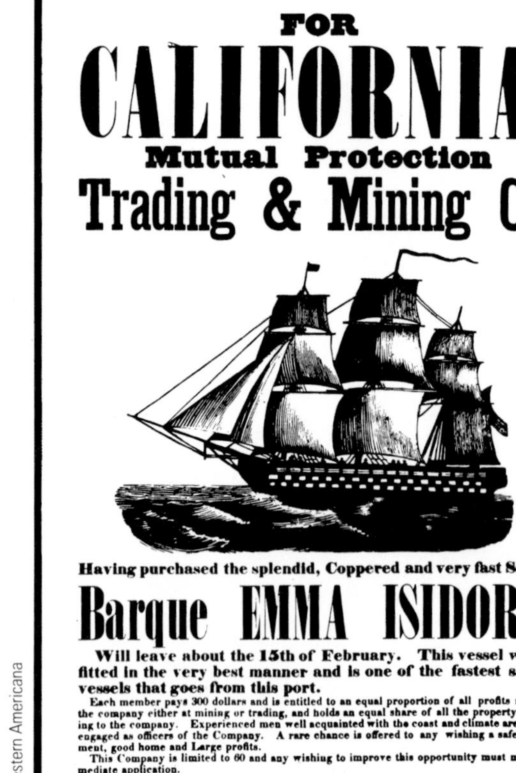

Peter Newark's Western Americana

Union & Central Pacific Railroad Line.
ONE CONTINUOUS EMIGRANT PASSAGE
—FROM—
OMAHA
TO STATION CANCELED.
Kelton. Marysville.
Palisade. Sacramento.
Battle Mountain Stockton.
Winnemucca. Lathrop.
Reno. Terminus So. Pacific R. R.
Truckee. San Jose.
Colfax. San Francisco.
NOT TRANSFERABLE
No Stop-over privileges given on this Ticket.
Baggage Checked only to Destination.
Whole 1876 Half 1877

Peter Newark's Western Americana

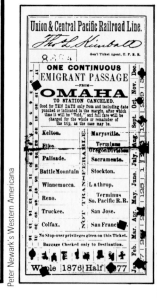

The discovery of gold in California in 1848 added to the emigration fever of the 1850s, and would-be migrants were tempted by special travel deals (above). First, however, a transatlantic port like Hamburg (below) had to be reached.

Archiv für Kunst und Geschichte

Ford Maddox Brown 'The Last of England'. By courtesy of Birmingham Museums and Art Gallery

This moving portrait of an emigrant couple captures the sadness of leaving. On the whole, emigrants tended to be young and active people. Most of them never returned to their native lands.

The mid-century exodus

The great mid-century emigration from Germany began about 1830 and persisted until 1854. There were three principal peaks: the early 1830s, the mid-1840s, and the mid-1850s, each triggered off by rising prices or poor harvests, or, to some extent, by a more definite view of America.

What people looked for in America at first was simply the negation of all the most unpleasant forces in German society: no kings, no taxation, no shortage of land. Goethe addressed an ode to America which praised the New World's lack of history: 'America, you have it better than our old continent. You have no crumbling castles, and are not torn apart by useless memories and pointless quarrels. Use your present well! And should your children become poets, let them not write about rulers, and robbers, and ghosts.'

Those who left were overwhelmingly the lower middle class: small farmers, merchants and artisans. At first the very poor did not join them since they did not have the money for the voyage or the clearly articulated ambition necessary to plan a new life. To some extent, those who left had seen their way of life destroyed by the new Germany. People found it easier to travel after the clearing away of tolls, frontiers and restrictions inside the German Confederation. Improved transportation on ships down the Rhine and the Main made the big ports more accessible.

But these same forces of modernization also destroyed many people's livelihood. They brought in a flood of cheap mass-produced goods which bankrupted the craftsmen and artisans. As textile machinery spread, possibly a quarter of the weavers in south-west Germany went bankrupt in the 1840s and starvation was a real danger to this ruined class. Among the farmers it was the custom in south-west Germany to divide the land between all the sons. Over the years the small farms grew smaller and smaller. Every agricultural improvement – the introduction of agricultural credit schemes, improved fertilizers, the cultivation of the potato – simply made it possible to start a family on an even smaller basis than the previous generation. Small farming became more and more marginal. One bad harvest would be a sufficient shock to uproot thousands and send them on their way to America.

Until the early 19th century the various governments had welcomed a growing population. Marriage, children, and even immigration were encouraged in all German states. But this official attitude changed abruptly as a series of economic depressions, a fear of overpopulation and of disturbances among the lower classes, made the authorities anxious to control the population. In Bavaria, Württemburg, and Hanover marriage legislation was tightened up. At first references were demanded proving the honesty and ability of the couple. By 1850 proof of one's status, such as the possession of lands or tools, was necessary to obtain a marriage licence. One result was that many young couples could find no way to start a family short of emigrating. (Another result of all this legislation was to push up the illegitimacy rate.) Most of this surplus population was at first absorbed inside Germany: people moved to the cities or to thinly populated agricultural areas. Prussia possessed both, and between 1824 and 1848 three-quarters of a million people moved to Prussia. But real emigration became a flood which did not abate. After 1848 even Prussia experienced a loss of population.

The lure of America

One reason was that every previous wave of emigration had led to more and more outposts of German settlers in America who sent back news and encouraged their relatives to join them. This meant that those who followed were taking less of a leap in the dark. Sometimes the authorities became alarmed by this loss of population and published accounts of Atlantic crossings blighted by disease and harrowing stories of the unemployment and exploitation that awaited those arriving in America. These official scare stories conflicted with letters arriving in villages and farms all over Germany, and it was the

Emigrants en voyage (below). In the cramped steerage diseases spread like wildfire, especially during rough weather when access to the fresh air on deck was restricted.

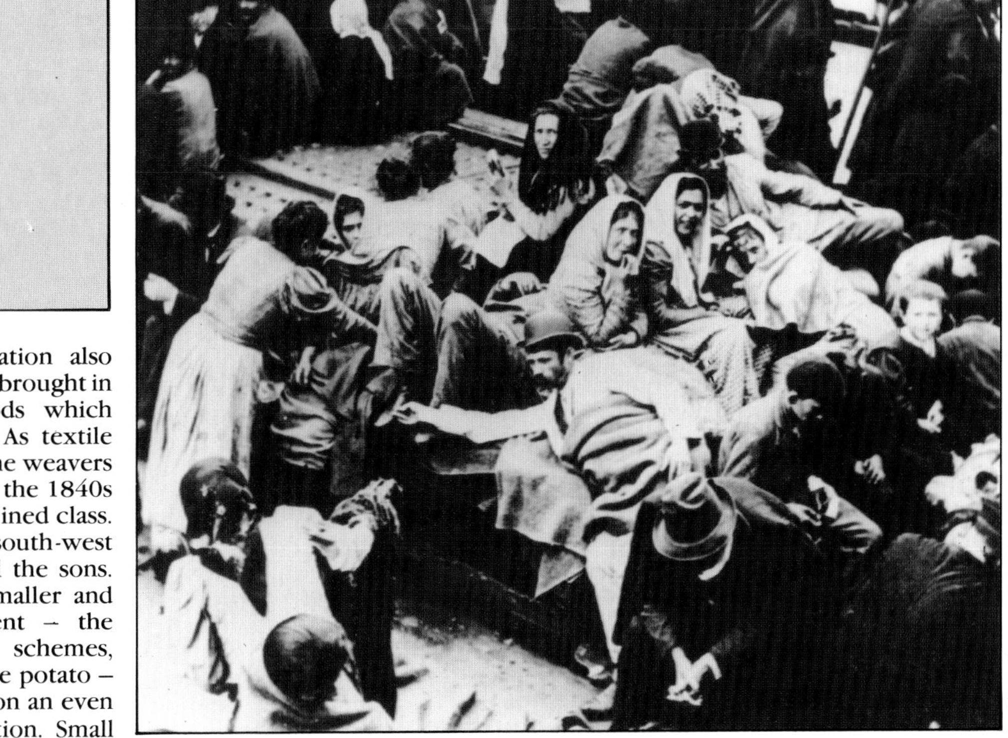

Archiv für Kunst und Geschichte

letters that were believed. Of course, the letters often exaggerated the prosperity of the American settlers. As the historian Heinrich von Treitschke wrote in his monumental *History of Germany:* 'The failures and the disillusioned were kept silent by shame, whilst the fortunate trumpeted their success to their kindred in Germany with all the pride of the self-made man.'

Certain books also encouraged this human flood. Gottfried Duden's *Report On a Journey to the Western States of America* appeared in 1829 just as the mass movement started. He announced that American political, social and economic conditions were superior to those in Germany, while the moral and intellectual qualities were much the same. Duden's work inspired hundreds of further articles and pamphlets and was one of the most influential books of its time. Duden even had doubts about having painted such a favourable picture of America and ten years later he published *A Self-Criticism Concerning His Travel Report, to Warn Against Further Rash Emigration.*

In 1845 the potato blight struck Europe: it appeared simultaneously across a vast area. From Galway to Trieste, from Portugal to Poland the stench of rotting potatoes drifted across the fields. Numerous rural areas in Germany were totally dependent on potatoes for food, and no one could explain or cure this disastrous disease. Gangs of looters began to attack food convoys on the road. Soldiers were called in to keep order on the streets of Cologne. In Berlin, farm wagons were attacked and plundered. The word 'communism' started to appear in newspapers all over Germany, and there were real fears that public order was disintegrating, fears that were intensified by the revolutionary fervour of 1848.

By now the poorer people were also leaving for America. The transport system was better, the fares were cheaper and the travel companies were larger and more efficient. Above all, there was active public and official encouragement. On balance, the state preferred an exodus to the New World to a hungry mob howling at the door.

The potato blight caused a massive migration in 1847, which was followed by a short pause as prices fell. But in the 1850s a further series of bad harvests triggered off an even larger wave of emigration. Between 1852 and 1854 over half a million people left Germany: one and a half per cent of the population. There were more single people, more poor people, more desperate people. For the first time the vast agricultural estates of east Prussia experienced emigration on a large scale. There were cases of entire villages uprooting and travelling in a mass to the Mid-West of America.

Sir Hubert von Herkomer 'Pressing to the West' Archiv für Kunst und Geschichte

The journey

In Germany, Bremen was the port that despatched the largest number of emigrants. Hamburg came a close second, and many found a passage via Liverpool. In the first half of the 19th century, crossing the Atlantic under sail took about six weeks; with adverse winds it could take much longer. At first many of these boats were simply cargo vessels whose owners realized that they could carry a profitable human cargo on the return journey. So a temporary deck was nailed across the cargo hold and hundreds of passengers, young and old, male and female, simply lay down in a 'promiscuous heap' and endured a wretched crossing. The hatches could not be opened during rough weather so ventilation was inadequate. The food which the captain supplied as part of the ticket was often inedible. Under these circumstances, outbreaks of cholera, dysentry and typhus were not surprising.

After 1848, American legislation forced improvements upon the shipping companies. Minimum standards of berth size and ventilation were specified, and it became possible to prosecute seamen who assaulted female passengers. The large-scale introduction of metal ships driven by propellors took place in the 1850s, though at first it was common for the propellor to drop off. For many years even the largest steamships carried auxiliary sail. By 1870 the westward crossing in a modern steamship could be accomplished in 14 days.

Once disembarked, not all the Germans struck out for the Mid-West. Many remained in cities and by 1860 there were over 100,000 Germans in New York, Chicago and St Louis, while Milwaukee also had large German communities where German businesses soon became household names. Eberhard Faber arrived in 1849 and began a pencil-making company. Henry Steinweg arrived in 1851 and began to manufacture Seinway pianos. Almost all the big names in American brewing were those of German

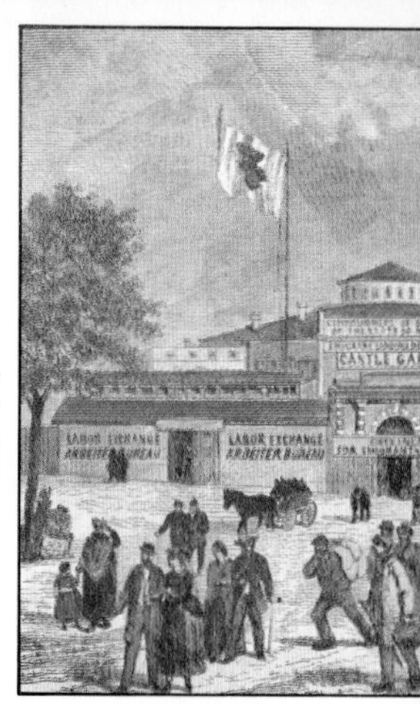

Archiv für Kunst und Geschichte

In the immigrant landing depot at Castle Garden (above) emigrants were 'sieved' through a series of health checks and quizzings by officials.

Bildarchiv Preussischer Kulturbesitz

This poster warns German girls against accepting jobs in America without making full enquiries. Female emigrants risked sexual harassment on the voyage, epecially in the steerage where privacy was impossible. On landing (left), unaccompanied women were liable to be sent back if they were suspected of being pregnant.

Only after passing through the 'nearest earthly likeness to the Final Day of Judgement' (right) were immigrants allowed to catch the ferry to Manhattan.

The Bettman Archive/BBC Hulton Picture Library

Reproduced by permission of the American Museum in Britain, Bath

The immigrants who followed the frontier westwards faced another endurance test as their wagon trains edged their way through hostile terrain.

immigrants – Pabst, Schlitz, Miller (formerly Muller) – who began to manufacture beer around Milwaukee in the 1850s.

The last great 'Auswanderung'

The American Civil War (1861–65), and the disruption in Germany due to Prussia's wars with Austria and France, caused the emigration figures to decline in the 1860s. But the Northern victory in the American Civil War was widely welcomed in Germany, and it was followed by a Homestead Act designed to attract new settlers. Then, as a result of German unification, conscription was introduced, which was particularly resented by small farmers: removing the sons to serve in the army made many farms unworkable. The combined effect was the biggest ever wave of emigration from Germany.

From 1871 to 1885, one and a half million Germans left their homeland. Ninety-five per cent went to the USA; two per cent to Brazil; one per cent to other Latin American countries; one per cent to Australia; and one per cent to Canada, Africa and Asia. Some German politicians declared that emigration on such a huge scale was a tragic loss to the German people. Unions and societies were promoted which would keep alive the language and the culture of Germany in their faraway settlements.

Archiv für Kunst und Geschichte

Henry Steinweg (above), founder of the famous Steinway piano company, did well in America. As farmers (right), his compatriots were equally successful and quickly earned a reputation for hard work and thrift.

Edimedia/Library of Congress

Peter Newark's Western Americana

The Society for the Protection of German Emigrants in Texas, known as the *Adelsverein,* actually purchased part of Texas in 1844. Several thousand German emigrants, under the leadership of the young Prince Karl of Solms-Braunfels, reached Texas in chartered ships where they set about building the town of New Braunfels. Unfortunately, they had not picked a particularly desirable piece of territory. Nothing could be grown, and then war broke out between Mexico and the United States for the control of Texas. Famine, disease and demoralization finished this project off, and it was widely condemned in the German press as a combination of swindle and dilettantism.

This situation only existed because Germany had no colonies. The French, the British and the Belgians could emigrate and still contribute to the greater glory of their homeland. A German emigrant was simply a loss to the country. Even after the unification of Germany, Bismarck did not pursue a very vigorous colonial policy: he seems to have regarded colonialism as an extravagance which could be ill afforded by a relatively new power such as Germany. Bismarck also instructed his civil service to publicize the dangers of emigration, and not to worry about emigrants who had got into difficulties. German officials should serve loyal citizens, not people who had left the fatherland.

Steerage passengers gaze joyfully at the Statue of Liberty as they enter New York (far left). A gift from the people of France, the statue was unveiled in 1886. The poem inscribed on its base warmed immigrants with its welcoming message: 'Give me your tired, your poor, Your huddled masses yearning to breathe free. The wretched refuse of your teeming shore.'

Settling down in the New World

Among the German communities of the Mid-West, German culture flourished. German farmers proved to be extremely successful in the New World, making shrewd judgements about the soil. They were also noticeably more frugal than the American pioneers in their methods of building and cultivation: having been brought up on marginal smallholdings in Germany, they wasted nothing. Daily newspapers, such as the *Cincinatti Volksblatt,* brought news of German hunting associations, gymnastic clubs, parades and festivals, as well as singing choirs and musical events, for the emigrants brought with them their love of music.

After 1870 most German–Americans were proud of their newly united fatherland, though they may have had no liking for Bismarck or the state that he had created. In America Germans were often treated with humorous condescension: patronized by the Yankees as amiable but ineffectual, a sentimental, beer-drinking, backward bunch of peasants. Now the emigrants could all take pride in the news that their homeland was clearly a world power, and Germans

For many immigrants the USA was not 'the golden door'. Here, free coffee is doled out to the poor of New York's Bowery district.

Edimedia/Library of Congress

in the New World became more self-confident and more assertive politically. In 1901 they formed the National German–American Alliance, to preserve German culture and to fight the spirit of Prohibition.

German social life placed a strong emphasis on beer gardens and beer festivals. They were central to the German concept of a good life, and Prohibition was seen by the Germans as an attack by the Yankees and the English Puritans on their favourite form of relaxation. By 1914 the German–American Alliance had two million members, and when the First World War broke out – and America was in theory neutral – these Germans believed it was their duty to redress the overwhelmingly pro-British bias of the American press. Initially this sparked off some anti-German irritation: 'Germany appears to have lost all her foreign possessions, with the exception of Milwaukee, St Louis, and Cincinatti!' as one newspaper put it in 1915.

Irritation turned to tragedy in April 1917 when America entered the war, fighting with Britain and France against Germany. All those millions of travellers who had made the *Auswanderung* – and their descendants – had to choose between their new home and the 'old country' they were now at war with. For most of them there was no choice. They had chosen the New World in preference to the Old, and now they had to live with the consequences of their move; during the First World War this meant putting up with some bizarre acts of anti-German prejudice. Towns and streets with German names quickly acquired new names. Sauerkraut became 'liberty cabbage' on many restaurant menus. The city of Boston banned the music of Beethoven for several months. And after the war, two states – Nebraska and Ohio – banned the teaching of German to schoolchildren below eighth grade, since this represented 'a menace to Americanism'. (These laws were declared to be unconstitutional in 1923.)

The ultimate ignominy took place in January 1920, when the Eighteenth Amendment enacting the Prohibition of Alcohol came into force. This seemed to spell the final subjugation of German culture to the spirit of English Puritanism. Many German–Americans who had seen the United States as a land of liberty wondered ruefully what had gone wrong.

A Kansas den of iniquity – the saloon – comes under fire from militant Prohibitionists. Such campaigns by temperance activists culminated with the enactment of the Prohibition law in 1920. This move was seen by many German–Americans, with some justification, as an assault on their traditional way of life.

IN THE BACKGROUND

Otto von Bismarck

In 1871 Johannes Brahms composed his Triumphlied *(Song of Triumph) to celebrate the proclamation of King William I of Prussia as German Emperor. Under the head of the Hohenzollern royal family, the German people – who had previously lived in 39 independent, warring states – was united to form the strongest military power in Europe. The man responsible for this achievement was not William I, but his Chancellor, Prince Otto von Bismarck. Bismarck united Germany by a policy of war abroad – both the Austrian and French empires were defeated on the road to Germany's unification – and iron political control at home. The 'iron chancellor's' methods had implications for future events; France longed to avenge her defeat, and German militarism was to make its mark on European history in two world wars.*

IN THE BACKGROUND

'The iron chancellor'

While Brahms was striving towards musical maturity his fragmented homeland, Germany, was unified through 'iron and blood' by a Prussian political genius: Otto von Bismarck.

Two figures dominated central European politics for most of the 19th century. Metternich (above) frustrated plans for a united Germany, but Bismarck (above right) later built a German Empire under Prussian control.

The diplomats who met in Vienna in 1814 (below) were staunch conservatives, dedicated to the restoration of the pre-Napoleonic status quo. They sought to maintain European stability by balancing the territorial rights of the great powers so that no single state could become so large as to have a de-stabilizing strength. But the compromises reached at Vienna were eventually swamped by the unstoppable tide of nationalist and democratic forces.

In 1815 Germany was a loose federation of 39 states. They owed a vague allegiance to Austria and her Hapsburg royal family as the strongest state in the German world. This world consisted of underdeveloped kingdoms connected by a few rivers and apallingly bad roads: Germany had no coherent economic or political shape.

By 1871, however, Germany had been transformed into the strongest nation in Europe. This new Germany was dominated by the state of Prussia and ruled by her royal family, the Hohenzollerns. Militarily, she had defeated Austria and France decisively. Economically, she was threatening to overtake Britain as the most industrialized nation in Europe. More than any other nation, the new Germany was the creation of one individual: Otto von Bismarck. His dramatic career changed the life of Europe forever and most Germans could not help but be impressed by his short-term success. Johannes Brahms believed that the two most important events of his lifetime were the completion of the *Bachgesellschaft Edition* (the publication of Bach's complete works) and the creation of the German state by Bismarck. Brahms usually travelled with a volume of Bismarck's speeches in his luggage which he would read for daily inspiration.

Metternich's 'patchwork' Germany

Bismarck's unification programme undid the careful arrangements of Prince Clemens von Metternich, the Austrian master-diplomat who had presided over the Congress of Vienna in 1814–15.

At this congress, Europe's senior statesmen had met to redraw the map of Europe after the final defeat of Napoleon. Four great powers – Britain, Russia, Prussia and Austria – dominated the proceedings. They were

Bildarchiv Preussischer Kulturbesitz

looking for a system of stability that would keep the lid on the potentially explosive ideas which the French army had helped to spread across Europe – nationalism and republicanism.

After all, reasoned Metternich, if every people demanded their own state, what would happen to the mighty Austrian Empire? Within its boundaries were Hungarians, Italians, Poles and Slavs, as well as the German-speaking Austrians who were the ruling class and provided the government bureaucracy. Austria's size and strength made her by far the most powerful country in the German-speaking world. From the capital, Vienna, the empire's main strength lay to the east and the south-east across Europe to the border with Russia, and south into Italy as far as Milan.

What we know as modern Germany was a complicated patchwork of kingdoms, principalities, free ports and duchies with one major power, Prussia, in the north. There had been over 300 of these tiny territories at the end of the 18th century and Napoleon's armies tore through them like a whirlwind. The very act of being invaded had awakened some of these states from their almost medieval existence. And the necessity of fighting the French had forced some of these rulers to co-operate with each other, and in some cases even to promise their people some kind of constitution. By the time the dust had settled and Napoleon had been despatched to St Helena in 1815 – the year of Bismarck's birth – Germany had been somewhat 'rationalized'. What Metternich proposed was a German Confederation of 39 separate states, ranging from the two superpowers, Austria and Prussia, to city-states like Frankfurt.

Of the many territorial changes made at the Congress of Vienna one was to have enormous significance: Prussia assumed control of the Rhineland and Westphalia. This meant that Prussia was now responsible for defending Germany's western border against the French. And as the 19th century progressed, the Ruhr with its vast coalfields became one of the most powerful industrial zones of Europe. The strategic and economic implications of the Rhineland were to be greater than anyone could have anticipated in 1815.

The year of revolution

Metternich knew that if Austria were to retain her role as the chief power among German-speaking countries, then Germany would have to remain divided. A Federal Diet (assembly) was set up in Frankfurt where representatives of the 39 members of the Confederation could meet to discuss common political and economic questions. Of course, Metternich's intention was that they would discuss how to keep change out of Germany, not how to unite it, and for 30 years the system worked well.

This system depended on strict censorship and a strong police presence, keeping a particularly close watch on student activities. So the German Confederation survived 1830 – a year of revolutionary activity all over Europe – with comparatively little damage. Although a few states introduced more liberal constitutions, Metternich's system endured until the next 'year of revolution', 1848, and then it fell apart quite dramatically.

In 1848 there were uprisings and disturbances all over Germany, while a revolution in Vienna even forced Metternich, the personification of established order, to flee from his own capital. Quite abruptly, Frankfurt became the site of an attempt to convene a German parliament. Through direct male voting, representatives from all of Germany were elected to discuss a German constitution. This was the newly emerging middle class expressing their desire for a more liberal style of government: about 200 of the representatives were lawyers and judges; 100 were professors and teachers; and there was just one peasant. The Frankfurt delegates were as liberal as Prussia was conservative.

The economic catalyst

Metternich's system had been destroyed by forces that not even the cleverest statesman could contain: industrialization and economic change. Because of the political tumult that convulsed continental Europe until 1815, industrialization occurred in Germany very late and very fast. The country had been divided not just into principalities, but also into numerous trading zones, criss-crossed with borders and frontier posts

Archiv für Kunst und Geschichte, Berlin

The meeting between King William I of Prussia and Otto von Bismarck in 1862 (left), at the height of a constitutional crisis, was to change the course of European history. Despite his status as Prussia's 'iron chancellor', Bismarck's attitude towards the king remained characteristically calculating. An aristocrat himself, he considered the royal family, the Hohenzollerns, to be 'no better than my own'.

In 1848 a wave of revolution swept across Europe. There were uprisings in every German state, and the fighting in Berlin (left) was particularly bitter and bloody.

charging a complicated tariff system, which impeded the flow of goods. With a view to administrative efficiency rather than a conscious desire to encourage commerce, Prussian civil servants gradually drew most of the German states into a free trade area, which was formalized as the *Zollverein* (customs union) in 1834. Austria remained outside the system to protect the trade within her own empire, so the effect was to draw the rest of Germany into an association with Prussia in the north.

But the economic innovation which did most to accelerate the industrialization, and eventual unification, of Germany was the building of the railways. And the railways revealed what a conservative country Prussia was, dominated politically and economically by the great landowners, the *Junkers*. The estates of the *Junkers* lay to the east of the Elbe – an area which is part of Poland and Russia today. There, the landowners' rule was absolute, and their sons became the officers of the Prussian army and the administrators of the civil service. (Bismarck's background and upbringing were classically *Junker*. He was despatched from the family estates to be educated in Berlin and though committed to state service of some kind all his life, he also maintained his responsibilities as a landowner.)

Initially, the *Junkers* were hostile to railways, just as they were hostile to all forms of modernization. But in the 1840s two obvious advantages of the railway system changed their minds: they realized that they could get their agricultural produce to wider markets more quickly, and therefore more profitably, and that railways could revolutionize the conduct of war, bringing enormous advantages to any army that had an extensive and swift transport system. As Germany was drawn together by economic forces, the great political questions that this process posed were: was it to be a federation or a centralized state? And what role would Austria play?

Bismarck takes the stage

At Frankfurt, in 1848, the liberal and professional classes tried to answer these questions. They drew up a constitution for all the German lands, and then offered the crown of German Emperor to Frederick William IV, King of Prussia, who refused it. He argued

The well-meaning men who met at the Frankfurt National Assembly in 1848 (right) were divided on the question of the shape the future Germany should assume. The principal split was between the pro-Prussian and pro-Austrian nationalists. Lacking internal unity, the Assembly was a government in name only. Without revenue or armed forces, it collapsed when Germany's counter-revolutionary rulers recovered their nerve. The way was then clear for Bismarck's strategy of achieving unity – not through elections and constitutions, but through 'iron and blood'.

Archiv für Kunst und Geschichte, Berlin

Bildarchiv Preussischer Kulturbesitz

During the 1850s Germany finally evolved into an industrial society. Wealth shifted from farming (above) to industry (right). This economic development did more to change the social order than revolution and debate.

that a king ruled by divine right and therefore could not pick up a crown offered by a parliamentary mob. This was a clear statement that Prussia was not interested in unification based on a liberal or broadly nationalist appeal, and Bismarck supported the old king's refusal.

At the Frankfurt parliament Otto von Bismarck first stepped on to the national stage and in his opening speech he presented himself as the most reactionary representative of a reactionary class. He was a huge man, powerfully-built, well over six foot, and he insulted most of the delegates with his opening remarks. When uproar broke out, he calmly stood and read a newspaper until it had subsided. It was a remarkable performance but it left a misleading image of Bismarck. He may have been a *Junker*, but he was hardly a conservative. As a political operator he was probably the most radical statesman of his time. What Bismarck possessed was an extraordinarily rapid and subtle grasp of any political situation. He could foresee the multiple implications of any initiative, and could improvise, or bluff, or threaten his way out of any situation. As an opportunist, he was a genius. He possessed total faith in his abilities, and he operated very much as a loner. He used political parties or politicians while they suited his plans, and then dropped them. He had no time for cabinets or colleagues or committees. He did not accept the chancellorship until he was certain he had total control, and then he used it ruthlessly, ordering the king around as sternly as any civil servant.

Bismarck in limbo

After his remarkable parliamentary dèbut at Frankfurt, Bismarck was given the job of representing Prussia at a re-convening of the German Confederation. As such, he was supposed to represent the policies of his seniors in Berlin, and report back to them. Instead Bismarck began to implement his own policies, sending reports off to Berlin instructing the government on what to do. Bismarck had seen through the whole tangled question of German unification and his solution was simple: Austria had to be totally ejected from the sphere of German politics and left to concentrate on her empire in south-eastern Europe. The way would then be clear for Prussia to take control of the German Reich – on her own terms.

But Bismarck's single-handed strategy was not

The Danish decision to make the duchy of Schleswig an integral part of Denmark presented Bismarck with the chance to take the first step towards uniting Germany. Bismarck made great political capital from Prussia's swift military victory (below).

Bildarchiv Preussischer Kulturbesitz

Christian Sell 'Battle of Königgrätz'. Historisches Museum Rastatt/Bildarchiv Preussischer Kulturbesitz

One by one, Prussia's rivals fell before her victorious armies. In 1866, it was the once-proud Austrian Empire that suffered, as the Hapsburg troops were routed in the Battle of Königgrätz (above).

appreciated by his political bosses and eventually he was sent off to languish as the Prussian ambassador to St Petersburg. 'I am being put into cold storage on the Neva,' he commented sardonically. In Berlin, the liberals and the conservatives argued endlessly about the future of Germany inside Prussia's parliament, but all through the 1850s things were going quietly Bismarck's way.

The Prussian railway network doubled its range; coal production virtually trebled; and the production of textiles, iron, and steel all increased in proportion. At the Great Exhibition of 1851 in London, one of the most talked about exhibits was a six-pound gun which had been cast by an iron-maker in the Ruhr, Alfred Krupp. Herr Krupp and his guns would also play an important part in Bismarck's plans for a greater Germany dominated by Prussia.

The currents of nationalism continued to erode the power of the Austrian Empire. In Italy, Count Cavour (the only statesman whose skill could compare with Bismarck's) made a pact with Napoleon III of France which enabled the Italians to throw Austria out of Lombardy, the richest province of the Austrian Empire. The defeat of the Austrian army at Magenta and Solferino was noted by Bismarck with interest.

Finally, in 1862, Bismarck's moment of destiny arrived. King William of Prussia, who had succeeded Frederick William IV in 1861, became locked in conflict with the Prussian parliament over the allocation of funds for the army. The king wanted to increase national service from two years to three, but parliament refused to pay for this. Neither side would give way, and the king was on the verge of abdicating until he was persuaded to consult Bismarck. Bismarc convinced the king that he could handle parliamen and also push through the army reforms; he emerge from this meeting as acting chief minister, ministe president, and foreign minister.

Iron and blood

Bismarck had virtually no knowledge of, or interest in domestic matters. What motivated him was a vision o the greater glory he could achieve for Prussia. On feature of the Prussian constitution that Bismarck understood very well was that parliament had no rea power over ministers. Ministers were appointed b the king alone, and they appeared before parliament t explain their policies. Parliament could exert financia pressure, but if the prime minister was determined t ignore parliament and he retained the confidence o the king, there was nothing that could be done.

In October 1862 Bismarck explained his policy t parliament: 'Prussia must gather together her forces conserving her strength for the favourable momen which has been missed several times already. Prussia's frontiers as drawn by the Congress of Vienna do no favour a healthy political existence. The grea questions of the day will not be decided by speeche and majority votes – that was the great mistake o 1848 – but by iron and blood.'

This policy was put into practice in three wars tha Bismarck initiated during the next eight years. Each had a specific political objective. Each was a work o political genius since each time Bismarck went to wa he had succeeded in isolating the enemy and neutralizing other forces so that they could not take

lvantage of the conflict. And each time he won. All ısmarck's strategy depended on was an army that ould not fail him, and in this respect he was rtunate: the Chief of the Prussian General Staff, elmut von Moltke, was a brilliant commander. He avelled incessantly, making maps wherever he went. e had carefully modernized and re-equipped his my. He had made extremely thorough preparations rough studies of communications, logistics, and – pecially – railway timetables. Elaborate plans were awn up to control the transport of troops, guns, ıpplies, wherever they might be needed in Europe.

In 1864 Bismarck went to war with Denmark, hich was trying to annexe the duchy of Schleswig. ısmarck presented himself as the defender of erman nationalism, and he persuaded the Austrian nperor Franz Joseph to join him. Obviously Austria ould not let Prussia invade alone, and so these two aders of the German people defeated Denmark. anz Joseph then proposed that the two principalities question – Schleswig and Holstein – should become dependent members of the German Confederation, ut Bismarck prevaricated, proposing that Schleswig e placed under Prussian administration, and Holstein nder Austria. A series of extremely complicated olitical wrangles followed, but the underlying principle was quite simple. Bismarck was trying to find a way of provoking a war with Austria.

Unification depended upon national pride in military victories, a pride that pervaded even children's games, as in 'Episodes in the German-Austrian War, 1866' (above). Victory over the French was crucial, and when Prussian troops entered Paris in 1871 (below), unification was complete.

It was a considerable gamble, because Austria had pulled herself together considerably since her defeats in Italy and indeed other European nations thought that the Austrians would win without difficulty. Saxony, Hannover, Bavaria and most of the secondary German states allied themselves with Austria, dimly realizing that if Prussia declared war on Austria she was in effect declaring war on all of Germany. This was to be the decisive battle and years later Bismarck recalled the moment before the conflict as 'the time when I was as close to the gallows as to the throne'.

On July 3, 1866, Prussia decisively defeated Austria on her own territory at the Battle of Königgrätz. The troops of both armies fought ferociously, but the planning and leadership of the Prussian campaign was far superior. Von Moltke's maps and timetables won the day. The rest of Europe was stupefied by the news of Austria's defeat, and Pope Pius IX uttered a famous cry: 'Casca il mondo!' ('The world is disintegrating!')

Having won his gamble, Bismarck took great care to limit the victory and to avoid humiliating Austria. The only territory lost by Austria was Venice, which Bismark had promised to the Italians in return for military support in the south. Franz Joseph had to agree to Prussia's annexation of the hostile German states she had marched through – Hannover, Kassel and Nassau, as well as the wretched territories of Schleswig-Holstein which had been in limbo ever since Bismarck and the Austrians had fought a war over them. The Austrian emperor had to agree to the dissolution of the German Confederation and to the setting up of a new confederation of German territories north of the Main, which was controlled by the Prussian Hohenzollern monarchy and which excluded Austria.

comic map of Europe 1871 (below) depicts apoleon III's France attempting to rebuff the designs of a belligerent Bismarck.

Bildarchiv Preussischer Kulturbesitz

Anton von Werner 'Die Kaiserproklamation 1871'. Schloss Friedrichsruh/Bildarchiv Preussischer Kulturbesitz

King William I of Prussia was proclaimed ruler of a unified Germany at Versailles in 1871. But he was unhappy at the ceremony because instead of 'German Emperor', he had wanted the less democratic title 'Emperor of Germany', and he left the hall without glancing at Bismarck (centre). The fact that all the dignitaries present are wearing uniforms is an indication of the fatally 'Prussian' character of the new Germany. Its brilliant military architect, von Moltke, stands to the left of Bismarck.

The final triumph

Bismarck's third and final war was waged with France in 1870. Again, this was preceded by an extremely complicated political wrangle in which Prussia proposed a Hohenzollern as a candidate for the throne of Spain. Napoleon III of France objected and Prussia seemed to back down, but at the last moment Bismarck succeeded in provoking a declaration of war by editing a telegram which described the French ambassador's meeting with the King of Prussia to make it appear as if the French had been grossly insulted. It was known as the 'Ems telegram' and it was a trivial pretext for a war that was to cast an extremely long shadow over the next 100 years.

Again, Europe expected a Prussian defeat. Bonaparte's invincible armies cutting across Europe were still a living memory and his nephew, Napoleon III, was believed to possess a similar style of military audacity. It was still not realized how carefully Bismarck and von Moltke had prepared for war, and just how confused the French politicians were.

France declared war on July 19, 1870. On September 1 Napoleon III and his army surrendered. A second French army of 173,000 men under Marshall Bazaine was beseiged at Metz, and they surrendered at the end of October. The city of Paris managed to hold out during a grim siege which lasted four months; by the end, the population of Paris was starving and hunting for rats and mice to eat. They surrendered in January, but two weeks earlier, on January 18, 1871, King William I of Prussia was proclaimed German Emperor in the Palace of Versailles: the symbol of France's glory was the site of her greatest humiliation. The purpose of this highly efficient war had been to draw the remaining southern German states into union with Prussia, and to formalize this new union as the German Empire. It was the final act which completed Prussia's annexation and domination of the rest of Germany. In Vienna, Brahms composed his *Triumphlied* (Song of Triumph) as a celebration of this most glorious moment of German history.

At no point was this new German state based on anything except Prussia's military strength. The institutions that make up a modern democracy – parliamentary debate, a free press, an independent judicial system – never had a chance to develop. After the 1863 elections, Bismarck fined parliamentary candidates who had criticized the government in their election speeches, and civil servants with the wrong opinions were dismissed. Bismarck believed that strong government consisted of rewarding your friends and obstructing your enemies. It was more than a coincidence that the only man of outstanding ability with whom Bismarck collaborated closely was the army Chief of Staff, von Moltke. From 1871 until 1945 Germany continued along the road first mapped out by Bismarck, and her history was decisively shaped by her military and industrial might.

IN THE BACKGROUND

Continental tourism 1800-1900

The development of civilian air travel in the mid-20th century opened up the world to the average person in the developed West. In the same way, the railway revolution of the 19th century created easier travel for the leisured middle classes. The idea of foreign travel in Europe was not new, but the Grand Tour of the 18th century was designed to broaden the outlook and educate a minority: rich, aristocratic young men. During the railway age, stations – once described as the cathedrals of the age – were built in all major cities; spa towns, like Baden-Baden or Bad Ischl, grew as people came to take the waters for their health or just to enjoy their social amenities; and the age of organized tourism began when Thomas Cook's travel company took people to exotic places like the Nile, but protected them from too much exposure to the rigours of 'abroad'.

IN THE BACKGROUND

'Wish you were here'

As a result of the railway bonanza, tourists (like Brahms) journeyed through the Continent in great numbers, gathering souvenirs and flocking to the playgrounds of the wealthy.

Travelling in Europe in the 19th century was exciting and uplifting enterprise, though someti the conditions of travel were so bad that voya often wished they had never embarked on exercise.

Modes of travel changed enormously through 19th century. In the early years before 1815, lo distance tours were mostly the pursuit of wea young men, who would embark on the Grand Tou a formal part of their education. Anybody who anybody (and that included Brahms in his turn) m the obligatory trip to Italy, by coach or horseback see the ruins of Pompeii, the leaning tower of Pisa, churches of Florence, and the canals of Venice – same places visited by millions of tourists today. Th trips through France to Italy were study-tours as m as sight-seeing holidays. Travellers went dutifull

William Powel Frith 'The Railway Station'. Royal Holloway College/Bridgeman Art Library

the museums, hired tutors for two or three-month ys to perfect their French and Italian, (though parently it was not uncommon for well-to-do folk in ner parts of Europe to use Latin as a means of mmunication!) or studied such subjects as art, chitecture or music. At the end of the trip they uld come home laden with pieces of masonry, tues, busts, lithographs and prints from the ruined ots they had seen.

The unstoppable spread of railways in Europe mpletely changed the character of travel. The first nch line opened in 1832, the first German in 1835, first Russian in 1838 and the first Italian in 1839. on, these short 'novelty' lines were followed by jor railways. By 1870 there were 65,000 miles of ck in Europe, and by 1910 the entire continental twork was all but complete. In 1871 the Alps were pierced for the first time by the eight-mile-long Mont Cenis tunnel and by 1888 it was possible to travel from Calais to Constantinople (Istanbul) by train. As mileages lengthened, ever higher standards of speed, comfort and reliability were set. Sleeping cars appeared in the 1870s, luxury transcontinental expresses – the most famous of which was the fabulous Orient Express – in the 1880s and refrigeration cars in the 1890s.

Wanderlust

The railways bridged the gap between town and country, contributing to an erosion of the fabric of traditional rural lifestyles, and they helped to make living conditions more uniform in the 19th century, regardless of cultural, linguistic and other national differences. So even as nationalism was producing a

The great railway stations were the 19th century's architectural answer to the cathedrals of medieval times, and they gave the cities of Europe a new focal point. There was something impressively universal about railway stations – symbolized by the great clocks that testified to the international synchronization of time. But in the distinctive hustle and bustle, each station maintained its own special atmosphere.

A. Solomon 'Departure of Diligence from Biarritz'. Royal Holloway College/Bridgeman Art Library

Horse-drawn traffic co-existed with the trains for travellers who went beyond important towns. Passengers had to endure a cramped discomfort that, nostalgia notwithstanding, was no match for the speed and ease of rail travel.

modern sense of identity with the state, nostalgia for the good old days of rustic innocence and a curiosity about other peoples' customs and ways of life were being aroused in urban populations. The railways offered a means of satisfying curiosity, nostalgia or just simple wanderlust. In Thomas Mann's *Death in Venice,* a highly-respected writer, Gustave Aschenbach, is seized with a romantic urge to travel:

> *Good, then, he would go on a journey. Not far – not all the way to the tigers. A night in a* wagon-lit, *three or four weeks of lotus-eating at some one of the gay world's playgrounds in the lovely south . . .*
>
> *So ran his thoughts, while the clang of the electric tram drew nearer down the Ungererstrasse; and as he mounted the platform he decided to devote the evening to a study of maps and railway guides.*

Armed with their Baedekers (back in 1829 an enterprising German publisher, Karl Baedeker, had published the first modern guidebook), the middle classes set off by rail in search of the sublime and the picturesque. They brought with them sketching equipment, butterfly nets and flower-pressing gear, as well as the weighty journals that would accommodate all their observations. By 1870 postcards 'wishing you were here' were being sent home and souvenirs – the inevitable cuckoo clock from Switzerland, the miniature Eiffel Tower (1889) from Paris – began to adorn the parlours of the travelled.

The great Austrian playwright, Arthur Schnitzle (1874–1931), had vivid memories of the proverbial pompous uncle who would bore his young nephew by reading aloud his travel diaries. 'He was very prou of them in spite of the fact that they contained nothin but dry reports of the sights worth seeing and all sor of railway and mailing dates, rather as in a Baedeke but without the compactness and precision of th useful book which his diaries were doubtless supposed to imitate.' These scrupulous litera records were in some ways the equivalent of th holiday snapshots of today.

The train transported Europe's wretched to the se ports where they could cross the Atlantic in the que for a better life in the New World. But as the emigran left Americans began to arrive in Europe to inspire th new stereotype of the Yankee tourist eager to see th place of his or her ancestors through rose-tinte spectacles. In 1865 Louisa May Alcott (author of suc best-sellers as *Little Women* and *Good Wives*) pai her first long-cherished visit to Europe as a companio to an invalid lady. Industrialization resulted in highe middle-class incomes generally and stocks and share including shares in family firms formed into priva companies, were a convenient way of providing fo huge numbers of 'ladies of means'. The comfortab avenues of Kensington in London, the villas of spas, th growing seaside resorts, the environs of Swis ountains and Tuscan cities welcomed such genteel d well-heeled patrons.

Louisa Alcott's experience is reflected in the count of vain Amy in *Good Wives* who 'does' Europe the company of a wealthy though crotchety aunt. r Amy, as for countless other women of her class, ris's Palais Royal was 'a heavenly place, so full of *jouterie* and lovely things that I'm nearly distracted cause I cannot buy them'. Her sail up the Rhine was erfect . . . the most romantic thing I ever saw'. The ths at Nassau were 'very gay' and 'so was Baden-den, where Fred lost some money (in the casino!)'.

Nice, the fashionable tourist's metropolis, 'haughty glish, lively French, sober Germans, handsome aniards, ugly Russians, meek Jews, free-and-easy nericans, all drive, sit or saunter here, chatting over e news and criticizing the latest celebrity who has rived – Ristori or Dickens, Victor Emmanuel or the ueen of the Sandwich Islands!'

National differences were perhaps more marked en than now. The southern countries were nowned for their classical beauty, romance and lour but left much to be desired in terms of eanliness and food.

It would be hard to exaggerate the impact of the ilways. Gone now was the old world of stage oaches and of more or less swift riding horses, of ckhorses and highwaymen. Apart from the surface nprovements of the late 18th century the roads of urope had not changed much since the days of the oman empire – Napoleon's army had travelled no ster than that of Julius Caesar. Strenuous efforts had en made to improve horse-drawn traffic by increas-g the number of horses; by harnessing teams of up to ght to pull heavy vehicles; and by making fresh orses available at staging posts along the roads for the nefit of travellers in a hurry. Even so, the ncomfortable stage coaches were thought of as ngerous, and with some justification. They went at n insane speed, accidents were numerous and no-one ompensated the victims. Furthermore, only a narrow central carriageway was paved on main routes: two carriages could not pass at the same time without a wheel plunging into the mud at the side of the road. Until the coming of the railways, travellers remained prisoners of a very limited range of choices. Though they could juggle routes so as to avoid a toll or customs post, they were still at the mercy of potholes and heavy rain which often made the going too difficult to be continued. In 1835 the average day's journey of a German mail coach was about 28 miles, a distance that a locomotive could cover in an hour.

Bildarchiv Preussischer Kulturbesitz

Railways were synonymous with glamour and progress, and their arrival, even in this Parisian suburb (above), was greeted with as much popular interest as the landing of Concorde might be today.

Organized travel

Thomas Cook, a Baptist lay preacher, began his organized tours in the 1860s, offering 'A Great

One of the great advantages of rail travel was the fact that, if you were a 'lady' or a 'gentleman', you did not have to endure the sight, smell and sound of people 'one did not normally meet'. A first-class compartment (left) offered all the civilities of home, while the lower orders, many of whom must have felt just as happy with the class segregation enshrined by the railway companies, jostled with each other on the hard uncompromising benches of third and fourth-class compartments (below).

A. Solomon 'Third Class'. British Transport Museum/Bridgeman Art Library

GOING OUT OF TOWN.
Mary. "If you please, Sir, Missus say you must find room for this in your Portmantel!"

For the 19th-century tourist, especially women, there was no such thing as 'casual wear'. Wherever you intended to be, appearances had to be kept up even if it meant transporting outrageously bulky items such as crinolines (left).

Arriving by steamboat (right). The locals have come down to meet the steamboat offering posies of flowers and a helping hand to the travel-jaded ladies, as well, no doubt, as their services as guides – an important source of extra income.

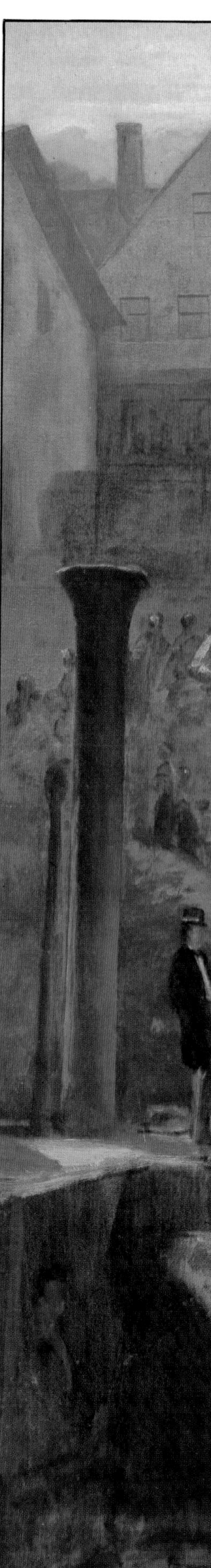

Circular Tour of the Continent'. Gone were the days when young men escaped their tutors and caught diseases, in Paris before learning a word of French (early travel books advised travelling with one's own linen to avoid catching 'the itch, venereal or any other disease' from murky unchanged inn-rooms). Instead, well-organized parties of intrepid couples and single young people could go anywhere – even as far as Greece or Egypt. Napoleon's invasions of the Far East had opened up great interest in these parts. But these were not the luxurious 'Orient Express' trips of later years: the parties were strictly teetotal, hymns were sung after dinner, and in the Holy Land, travellers slept in tents.

For those who preferred not to risk life and limb in these more exotic spots, journeying through Europe presented more sedate attractions mid-century. Half the reason to travel in Europe was to enjoy society – a fact almost as important as the views of mountains or the delights of the museums. A most popular area for holidaying in Europe was the Low Countries. It offered better hygiene and some cultural centres of note. The condition of the roads was much better than in Germany, making travel in a private carriage less hazardous. Holland appealed because of its small size, the diminutive, cleanly aspect of the villages, and the good standard of the most modest taverns. In the main cities, there were Inns that were run for English people: the Golden Ball at Leyden, the Queen of Hungary at the Hague, the King's Head at Middleburg, Mrs. Cator's in Wine Street, Rotterdam. Amsterdam of course attracted a large number of tourists, from the 17th century onwards; it was the next largest city after London and Paris, and being a port was well stocked with gifts: tiles, maps, books, gemstones, tulip bulbs.

Of course there was a certain fear in the air in the first half of the 19th century that Napoleon could spring up anywhere in Europe. This added an excitement and piquancy to any trip abroad. Half of Europe seemed to be at arms – the Prussians, the French and Austrians, at various times. Thackeray's *Vanity Fair* contains a wonderful description of the terrors in Brussels when the army was caused to fly by Napoleon's manoeuvres, with tourists, camp followers, army families, all charging about the city, with the sound of cannon echoing in their ears, and a universal urgency to find horses for their carriages. It seems strange to us that people would even risk going abroad at all at such times, but it only shows how the scale of war has changed. People would still travel around Europe, bumping into a localized spot of bother, but undeterred by it. And after the hostilities dormant battle grounds were picked over by tourists searching for war relics.

Travelling first class

How did a wealthy family travel to such a spot as this in the 19th century? If English, they would first cross the Channel in a steamboat, probably taking their own coach (crested) with them, and a good supply of servants: coachmen, ladies' personal maids, children's nurses, and so on. Through the northern countries, steamers plied the rivers, from Rotterdam, or Cologne, on which these vehicles would be taken aboard. Then they would be moved ashore, and the rest of the journey continued in privacy. Gradually, journeys between big cities were undertaken by train, but the links between outlying places were still very poor. Either one went by private coach, or by local open wagon (very dusty to sit in) or on foot – as Brahms did many times.

Once established in a hotel in the town chosen as the holiday centre, like Weimar, the Englishman or other traveller of note would leave his card with his local consul. This would serve as an introduction to the notables in the town and as a gentle hint: a notice might appear in the society column of the town newspaper announcing the arrival of the distinguished travellers, and that in turn would ensure that the locals would lose no time in calling, leaving their cards or invitations to soirées, balls, intimate dinners, or visits to the opera box.

During the day, the travellers would walk about the lakes or along the river's edge, like the Rhine, depending on their location, engage in simple pastimes such as sketching, reading, or for the men, shooting parties. If the stay was to be prolonged, it was often the custom until late in the 19th century, for a party of travellers, a family or companions, to move into lodgings (the cost of hotels was prohibitive, even for the wealthy) and to dine either *à table d'hôte* in the hotel, or in the private homes of new friends in the course of socializing.

This system of travelling sounds very grand, but it was not reserved exclusively for the aristocracy. Other people of note would travel in very much the same way. George Eliot, the well-known English novelist, describes a stay at the Erb-prinz, a grand hotel in Weimar. In 1854 she wrote:

The lines of houses looked rough and straggling and were often interrupted by trees peeping out from bits of garden. At last we stopped before the Erb-prinz, an inn of long-standing in the heart of the town, and after some delay through the dreamy doubts of the porter whether we could have rooms before the 'Herrschaft' had departed, we found ourselves following him along heavy-looking corridors and at last were ushered into a room which overlooked a garden for all the world like one you may see in many an English village at the back of a farmhouse.

George Eliot found Weimar 'more like a market town than the precinct of a court'. She and her companion soon moved into lodgings, at a cost of £2.6s per week, including wine and washing.

Then as now, travelling in northern Europe was always a problem owing to the weather: rain made the roads impassable, and thick Victorian clothing was not very easily dried out and cleaned. Female travellers often succumbed to influenza and worse – not surprisingly, for although they wore many petticoats and overgarments, the style in fashion always called

Spitzweg 'Landing off a Steamboat'. Joachim Blauel/Artothek

Tourism was a serious pursuit in the 19th century and Baedeker guidebooks giving advice on travel and sights were pored over enthusiastically by tourists (below).

Bildarchiv Preussischer Kulturbesitz

Thomas Cook (right) was born in Derbyshire of humble background. A Baptist lay preacher and temperance worker, he became, through his celebrated travel company, the archetypal self-made man of the 19th century. The Great Exhibition gave him his first major business success, but by the 1880s he owned steamboats on the Nile and the funicular railway that took tourists up the flank of Vesuvius. Cook's success was not only due to good timing and tremendous entrepreneurial imagination. His clients appreciated the fact that on his well-organized and inexpensive tours they were protected against the more awkward and inconvenient rigours of 'abroad'.

The Mansell Collection

for low-cut fronts to their dresses, and their footwear was always impractically light.

When Brahms set out for a walking tour in the Rhineland, his mother wrote with the usual admonitions, for Brahms took only a stout stick and a rucksack on his back:

Such steep rocks! How easily you could fall there! I tremble when I think of it. Your chest is strong of course, but one can overdo things with so much climbing . . . Therefore Johannes dear, please take care of yourself and for heaven's sake don't go out in a thunderstorm.

Baden-Baden

Sometimes, the wealthy traveller would have a surfeit of socializing in the princely towns of the Lowlands, Germany or Austria; then he would take himself off to a spa, for a ritual rest and cleansing out after the excesses of balls, operas, and late-night dinners. The most well-frequented of these was Baden-Baden. Situated on main routes between Paris and Vienna, Russia and Spain, it was ideally placed to attract all the nobility of Europe.

Brahms's great friend Clara Schumann had a house at Lichtental, close to Baden-Baden, which she bought in 1863 and kept as a holiday home until 1879. Brahms himself, like many another visitor to the spa, took lodgings, with a Frau Becker, from where he would walk in the surrounding woods, work until lunchtime, then eat out, either at the 'Golden Lion', or, when he had company and was prepared to spend a little more money, at the 'Bear'. In the afternoons, he would go over to Clara Schumann's and often stay there for supper before returning to his rented rooms.

For the more wealthy patrons of the spa, the casino had been built in 1821. It was the most ornate and long-established gambling house in Europe – the interior was decorated by the designers of the Paris Opéra – and helped give Baden-Baden its name as

Greetings from Monte Carlo (right). Such postcards travelled home by mail train, and they revealed not only the experiences of the privileged tourist, but the advent of mass literacy.

The Mansell Collection

Europe's 'summer capital'. The casinò had beautiful gardens with fountains set round it, and every gambling room was decorated in a different style, from the Renaissance to the Empire.

Besides the entertainment there were the spa watering rooms and baths which had been laid out originally by the Roman Emperor Caracalla. The hot springs came from a depth of 6500 feet, the hottest in Europe. The Friedrichbad, the most imposing of the spa buildings, was erected in 1869, and opened when the gambling halls were closed in 1870, with the foundation of the German Empire: this was an effort to revive tourism in the town, redirecting it towards medical recuperation instead of the casinos.

Baden-Baden has always maintained a very aristocratic air: Queen Victoria went there frequently with her family, as did Kaiser Wilhelm I, who summered there for 12 consecutive years from 1871. The town had a considerable artistic presence, for it had its own opera house in the Goetheplatz, which Hector Berlioz opened in 1862 with his opera *Beatrice and Benedict,* on 9 August.

Bad Ischl

Another favourite spa in 19th-century Austria was Bad Ischl, near Vienna. It was the summer resort of the ill-fated Emperor Franz-Joseph (1830–1916) who loved to go hunting in the woods and hills surrounding the town. When Brahms stayed there, as he did many times in the final years of his life, he would take cheap lodgings on a mountain slope overlooking the river, on the outskirts. He would walk into town for a good meal at the Hotel Kaiserin Elisabeth, or sit about in Walter's coffee-house to read the papers. In this popular resort you could enjoy boating and mountain strolls by day, with music, theatre, card games and plenty of chances to flirt and gossip by night. And if you travelled to Bad Ischl in the uniform of an officer the train fare you were charged was half price.

Bad Ischl is part of Austria Salzkammergut, (literally 'salt chamber', after the important salt mines worked there since 1570). It is still very much a tourist centre. The chief city is Salzburg, where the Mozart festival takes place every year. (Brahms had a dear friend, Theodor Billroth, who had a summer retreat at St. Gilgen, on the lake, the birthplace of Mozart, and he would take a train or boat trip often during his summer months to visit his friend.) There were some very grand hotels at Bad Ischl, like the Post, or the Hotel Austria, that soon attracted all the crowned heads of Europe. As the author Joseph Wechsberg described it: 'My mother once asked my father to take her to Ischl for "the season" and he sadly shook his head. Impossible, he said, he could not even get a room there. In Ischl a 21-carat duchess was glad to have a small *Kabinett* without a bath. The VIPs whom the Emperor did not want to have at his villa were put up at the leading hotel, the Post'.

A spot further east in Czechoslovakia was another favourite. Karlsbad is no longer visited as once it was – the spa continues at the small town of Karlovy Vary. It had a long association with artistic folk: Goethe went there for 13 years in a row, followed by Beethoven, Turgenev, Gogol, Tolstoy, Schumann, Paganini, Wagner, Strauss, and Brahms, who came there in the last year of his life suffering from cancer. He was not cured: he returned to Vienna and died there seven months later. The hotel he stayed in, the House Brussels, was one of the well-known social spots of the spa town, and he went several times to a box in the Burg theatre in the evenings.

Beyond the Alps

For those who still wanted to travel further south, there were hazards to be encountered crossing the Alps, long after the railway network had effectively

Taking the waters in a Swiss spa in 1873. The curative properties of natural spring waters have long been celebrated. In the 19th century, however, immersal was a very serious and prolonged affair, to judge by the concentration of the water-bound chess-players, the serious demeanour of the tea-bearer and the literary studies of other occupants of the pool.

The Mansell Collection

The casino at Monte Carlo in 1890 (above). In opulent surroundings, immense sums changed hands, while 'cocottes' (loose women on the make) hung around in all their finery, ready to escort some momentarily rich gambler home.

spanned the northern towns. The passes through the mountains still had to be negotiated on foot or with mule trains, right up until the 1870s. Dickens describes the journey through the Simplon Pass in *Little Dorrit:* the family set off on mules and spent the night at the convent of Saint Bernard, at the top of the pass. It was an arduous and cold journey, moving slowly through swirling mists, and slow indeed. At least the convents and monasteries that offered hospitality to travellers provided simple food and clean lodgings: the inns in the mountain villages were notoriously filthy. Sometimes families still travelling in private coaches would have them dismantled and carried, piecemeal, through the mountain passes, so that they could continue on their way south in customary style. This was common practice through the pass at Mont Cenis, the route from Lyons to Turin. Alternatively, the carriage would be left on the northern side, awaiting the travellers' return.

Once the railway network cut through the mountains, it became much easier to travel to the south of France and further on to Italy. That strip of coast, the Riveria, had been successful as a seaside resort for many decades, mainly for a small group of writers who liked to spend the winter there. No one of course took the sun. The idea of beach holidays and suntans was almost unknown until after the First World War. It was Coco Chanel, the French dress designer, who made it fashionable to get brown. Italy ceded Nice to France in 1861, and from then on the area grew in popularity as a winter retreat. Another major factor in its rise to fame was the closure of the casino at Monte Carlo. The English presence was always very considerable: the first hotel, the German-owned Hotel des Anglais was built in the early years of the 19th century, and in 1882, the locals raised the finance to build a 'Promenade des Anglais' along the sea front. Then in 1883, the first 'train bleu' run by La Compagnie International, the Calais-Paris-Nice Express, arrived on the coast in November and set the area on the map as a holiday resort.

Tourism in Europe continued to be an elegant business, right up until the end of the Second World War. Only then did ordinary people have the leisure time – and the spare money – to enjoy Europe as the well-heeled class had done before. But tastes in holidays changed completely. Fewer people went on robust walking holidays, so much a feature of Victorian life, nor had they the need to purge their systems at the spa towns either, since over-feeding and rich diets had become the style of the past. Sport activities replaced cultural trips. The measured pace of the mid-19th century travellers had gone forever.

The well-to-do went to Nice to stroll along the Promenade des Anglais (right) and enjoy, but not be exposed to, the Mediterranean sunshine. Suntans were not at all fashionable – only workers had rough tanned faces – until after the First World War.

THE GREAT COMPOSERS

Gustav Mahler

1860-1911

Gustav Mahler was the last of the great symphonic composers to be based in Vienna. He was Jewish, and all his life had to battle against anti-Semitism, which undoubtedly motivated some of the virulent attacks against him. He had the added disadvantage of coming from a humble background – his father was a publican – but Mahler's family recognized and encouraged his talent. Mahler's importance as a conductor was soon apparent – his time as Director of the Vienna State Opera was tempestuous, but the company was then at its most brilliant. However, his greatness as a composer took longer to recognize: Ralph Vaughn Williams, the British composer, once referred to Mahler as 'a tolerable imitation of a composer'. Today, however, Mahler's greatness is readily acknowledged and his symphonies, especially in their use of the human voice, are seen as works of true genius.

When Mahler wrote that 'the symphony is a world', he was describing his own musical output since, apart from song cycles, he wrote little else except symphonies. In these works, he wanted to express all human emotion and experience; and, as the Composer's Life *describes, Mahler experienced in his own life extremes of emotion that are readily apparent in his compositions. The* Listener's Guide *analyzes Mahler's symphonies through those movements chosen by the Italian director, Visconti, for his film of Thomas Mann's book,* Death in Venice. *It is possible to examine in detail only a small part of Mahler's symphonic output, but even a few examples would be sufficient to highlight his genius. For much of his musical life, Mahler was based in Vienna, for long the musical capital of Europe.* In the Background *describes how Vienna's days as political capital of the Austro-Hungarian empire were numbered; the atmosphere of* fin de siècle *was expressed for posterity by the artists of the Secession, led by Gustav Klimt.*

Österreichische Nationalbibliothek

COMPOSER'S LIFE

'The symphony is a world'

Mahler, a Jew living in a city poisoned by anti-Semitism, fought his way through a life punctuated by devastating blows. But in both his conducting and his extraordinary music his innovative and restless genius emerged triumphant.

Gustav Mahler was born to a Jewish family on 7 July 1860, in Moravia (now a province of Czechoslovakia). He was the second of 12 children born to Bernhard and Marie Mahler, five of whom died at an early age. Mahler was not exempt from the troubled legacy of the Jews living in the Austro–Hungarian empire, and the 19th-century persecution of the Jews had directly affected his family. Under the infamous *Familiengesetz* law introduced by Metternich, only the eldest son of a Jewish family was free to marry. Due to this law, Gustav's own father Bernhard had, in official terms, been born illegitimate – which was a great social burden to carry in those times.

Through sheer determination in the face of official interference and discouragement, Bernhard had managed to build up a comfortable liquor business (one of the few trades open to the Jews) and give the family a secure financial standing. A harsh and brutal authoritarian, Bernhard always insisted on a good education for all his children and, when young Gustav first displayed great musical talent, this was recognized and encouraged. By the age of six his vocation had already been decided upon and from that time on great sacrifices were made by the entire family to ensure Gustav's steady progress.

Österreichische Nationalbibliothek

Marie Hermann, (above) married Bernhard Mahler in 1857. But he proved to be a brutal and domineering husband and her marriage was a sad and loveless one. Gustav (right, aged six) was devoted to his maltreated mother and was deeply saddened by her death in 1889.

Youth and education

In 1874 a local administrator, Gustav Schwarz, heard the 15-year-old Mahler and was immediately convinced of his potential. Eager to help nurture the young boy's talent, he persuaded Bernhard to send his son for proper training at the Vienna Conservatory. Though this meant a complete break from his home in Iglau, his father realized the importance of thorough training and let the boy go. Arriving in Vienna in September 1875, Mahler quickly blossomed and threw himself into the hectic musical life of the city. In his three years there as a student, he wrote a number of compositions for piano (virtually all of which he destroyed later in life) and was soon in trouble for his radical ideas, pugnaciousness and unpunctuality.

Archiv für Kunst und Geschichte

Mahler's first home (above) was in the village of Kaliště, Bohemia where he was born in 1860. But before the year was out the family moved to a larger house in the more prosperous town of Iglau.

In 1878, the year he graduated, Mahler began work on his first mature work, *Das klagende Lied* (The Song of Lament) and enthusiastically took up the lifestyle of a composer. For two years he was supported by his family as he attempted to compose, but the isolation and privation led to depression, disillusionment and a complete dissipation of his energies. This was a crucial period for Mahler, for it proved he was not psychologically equipped to deal with such a solitary vocation. He decided to pursue the idea of becoming a conductor and by mid-1880 he had taken the first step to that end.

The start of a career

By the summer of 1880, Mahler had made his début in Bad Hall, near Linz, and his success there led to a position in Laibach (now Ljublijana), in the province of Carinthia (now Yugoslavia), for the 1881–2 season. His career had begun.

His next position took him, in early 1883, to the Stadttheater in Olmütz where his sure instincts, superhuman zeal and clever handling of the slenderest resources paved the way to his first appointment to a professional opera company. This was in Kassel, in Prussia, for the 1883 season. But the renowned Prussian mania for petty bureaucracy soon had Mahler embroiled in numerous disputes. Irritated by officialdom, the young conductor lasted only two of his three contracted seasons. In 1885 he moved on to Prague, then to Leipzig in 1886 with little to show for his Herculean labours. But at least while in Kassel he embarked on his first major love affair, with a young singer in the company, called Johanna Richter, and this had inspired him to write the first of his *Lieder eines fahrenden Gesellen* (Songs of a Travelling Companion), setting his love poems to music.

While his position as junior 'Kapellmeister' at the Leipzig Stadttheater was a boon for Mahler, his term there was clouded by scandal. In the summer of 1887 he was asked by Baron Carl von Weber, grandson of the composer Carl Maria von Weber, to complete a series of comic operatic sketches entitled *Die drei*

Archiv für Kunst und Geschichte

Pintos (The Three Pintos) which the great man had left in disarray on his death in 1826. This was a great honour and Mahler applied his customary zeal to the work. But a disturbing side-effect soon manifested itself – the young man became entangled in a torrid affair with Baron von Weber's wife, Marion. In a climate of increasing pain and difficulty, Mahler finished the opera, and it was later accorded success on the stages of Europe in 1888. But the price was high; an elopement was abandoned only at the last moment, and the Baron himself, unable to bear the emotional strain of the situation, had a long-lasting breakdown.

This scandal hurt Mahler and indirectly led to his resignation from Leipzig in 1888. But within a few weeks he was offered the position of new Director at the Royal Budapest Opera. This was a dazzling appointment for the 28-year-old Mahler and he was quick to prove equal to it.

The thrill of the appointment in Budapest, and his initial success with audiences, the opera company and music critics, was soon to be overshadowed. In February 1889 his father died, leaving Mahler with a heavy burden of financial and family worries. On top of this, his critics both inside and outside the opera were becoming hostile towards some of his innovatory work, and he was soon publicly attacked for every deficiency, whether or not it was actually his fault.

After a fitful summer break spent putting the finishing touches to his First Symphony, Mahler's life

Tasting the new crop's wine at open-air wine shops (left) was as popular a tradition in Vienna in the 1880s, when Mahler was there, as it is today. Mahler studied at the Vienna Conservatory from the autumn of 1875 to the summer of 1878 then, after a series of short-term jobs, was appointed junior 'Kapellmeister' at the Leipzig Stadttheater (below) in 1886. But personality clashes with other conductors there and involvement in a major romantic scandal forced him to resign within two years.

Archiv für Kunst und Geschichte

Archiv für Kunst und Geschichte

In 1890 Mahler met and became close friends with Natalie Bauer-Lechner (above). She was well aware of his genius, unlike the general public or music critics who, in the previous year, had met his First Symphony (title page below) with considerable derision. The cartoon (right), printed shortly after the première with a one-word caption meaning 'effect', shows how little his adventurous composition was appreciated.

Österreichische Nationalbibliothek

was shattered by the deaths of both his mother and his favourite sister, Leopoldine. With his sorrow scarcely contained, Mahler had to wind up his family's affairs in Iglau and re-house his younger brothers and sisters. The year of 1889 was perhaps the unhappiest of the composer's life.

Romantic interlude

In 1890, his life took on a happier note. In the autumn Mahler met Natalie Bauer-Lechner.

A young violinist, Natalie was recovering from a broken marriage when she and Mahler met. A tall and not unattractive woman, she proved to be attentive, inquisitive and devoted almost to a fault. She kept a journal relating every piece of information regarding Mahler during the years of their 'intimacy'. A scrupulous and gifted chronicler, her records are invaluable in giving later generations a true insight into Mahler's creative genius. It is true that the conductor was often irritated by her devotion and constant attentions, but he recognized her qualities. He had a real fondness for her and spent many summers with her and his sister Justine. Yet sadly for Natalie his emotions were never as passionately engaged as hers.

Also in November 1890 he came into contact, for the first time, with Johannes Brahms. Dragged unwillingly to see Mahler conduct *Don Giovanni*

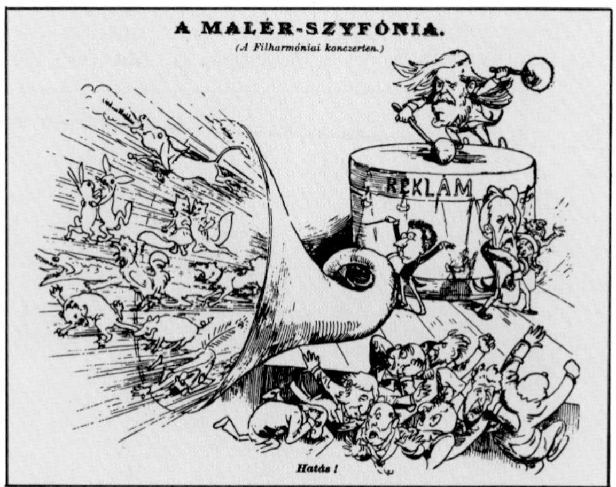

while in Budapest, Brahms was immediately won over by Mahler's interpretative genius, crying out 'Bravo' from his box. In later years, Brahms was to do much to help Mahler's career, though he never liked his compositions.

The road to fame

By the spring of 1891 things had come to a complete deadlock at the Royal Opera in Budapest, and Mahler's departure was only a matter of time. His new appointment as conductor with the Hamburg Opera was finally confirmed, and he took up the position with relish. He was to spend six years there and, although he was to battle continually with the Opera administration for higher standards and with German critics who were disdainful of innovative methods, it was a period when he finally assumed his position in the front rank of contemporary conductors. It was also a period during which he won the friendship of many great and famous musicians, such as the conductors Hans von Bülow and Willem Mengelberg.

The 1892 season gave him particular pleasure because he had the personal satisfaction of meeting

Archiv für Kunst und Geschichte

Bildarchiv Preussischer Kulturbesitz

'One cannot imagine how beautiful and animated this city is', wrote Mahler to his sister (with him, right) when he arrived in Hamburg (left) in March 1891. He was about to take up his most prestigious post yet, as first conductor with the Hamburg Opera company. His six years there were important and creative and included working with Tchaikovsky on his opera* Eugene Onegin. *Some of the stage sets for it were spectacularly grand (as below), but the opera itself was only a moderate success.

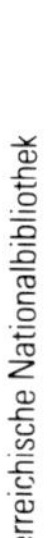

Österreichische Nationalbibliothek

Anton Brioschi 'Stage design for Eugene Onegin: a ballroom'. Österreichische Nationalbibliothek

Tchaikovsky. After conducting the rehearsals of Mahler's opera *Eugene Onegin,* Tchaikovsky further honoured Mahler by staying to watch the première.

The following year also saw the flowering of Mahler's long friendship with Richard Strauss, a young man who was doing precisely what Mahler had always dreamed of by winning ecstatic reviews for both his conducting and his compositions. By contrast, Mahler's own composing was going slowly – he had just finished his Second Symphony – and his reputation in the field of composition was slight.

Emotional upheavals

As if Mahler and his family had not sustained enough blows already, a new misfortune beset them in early 1895. After a period of relative domestic peace, when his sisters Justine and Emma shared his Hamburg home with him, there came the tragic and unexplained suicide of their brother Otto in Leipzig. Gustav was so deeply affected by this loss that he never mentioned it for the rest of his life. And only after his own death did his widow, searching through an old trunk, find three symphonies and a collection of *Lieder,* all written by Otto, which Gustav had never been able to bring himself to look at again.

Perhaps it was this deeply-buried sorrow which expressed itself in the sudden and tempestuous affair he started later that year with a new young singer at the opera house, Anna von Mildenburg. Passionate and ill-concealed, the relationship was soon common knowledge throughout the company. The tortuous affair, which went to the brink of what would have been a suicidal marriage, dragged on for over a year, fed by Anna's jealous possessiveness and Mahler's inability to make a clean break.

The relationship finally came to an end when Mahler left Hamburg for a new position in mid-1897. He had been angling for the post of Director at the Imperial Vienna Opera for over a year, as his relationship with the Hamburg director Bernhard Pollini had been deteriorating drastically. He wanted nothing more than to leave the city which had witnessed disastrous attempts to introduce his own music (not one ticket had sold for the première of his Second Symphony), and scenes of open humiliation in front of his own company by Pollini, who loudly insinuated that his prized conductor was actually incompetent.

A break with the past

Early in 1897, the job in Vienna became available. But Mahler's appointment was only secured after he had resigned from Hamburg and had also taken the unusual step of converting to Catholicism. Mahler, who was not an orthodox Jew, realized that he would never otherwise get the Vienna appointment, anti-Semitism being rife in official circles, and he was willing to make the change. But although he was a deeply religious man, he never became a practising Catholic.

Vienna was the opera capital of the world at the time, and this appointment was a crowning achievement in Mahler's public career. His first season there was one of unqualified triumph, and with his fanatical dedication and inexhaustible dynamism he reversed the previous decline in performing standards. He remarked to a colleague at the time, 'I am hitting my head against the walls, but the walls are giving way . . .'. So successful was he that by the end of spring 1898, when Hans Richter resigned from the post of Director of the Vienna Philharmonic, Mahler was invited to replace him.

Trials and tribulations in Vienna

But after the initial wave of success, public response began to change, and the old problem of critical publicity reared its head. At first it didn't concern Mahler as he was enjoying capacity audiences for his productions, and even for his stagings of complete, uncut Wagner operas (a rarity at this time). But a virulent and libellous smear campaign was mounted in the two anti-Semitic Viennese papers. He was even referred to as 'that dwarf Jew'. Sworn to dignified silence by his employers during the subsequent court case, Mahler could only fume. Even his new summer retreat at Wörthersee, where he completed his Fourth Symphony, and his hiring of brilliant new singers such as Franz Naval, couldn't compensate for the indignities he had suffered.

Events reached a climax in the winter of 1900–1, with the Viennese première of his First Symphony being roundly hissed and booed, and many of his opera productions being savagely attacked by the critics. Undoubtedly suffering from tension caused by those setbacks in his life, Mahler became seriously ill in the spring, and needed a long convalescence.

Archiv für Kunst und Geschichte

The Vienna Opera House (above) was the home of one of the world's greatest opera companies and Mahler was delighted when he became director in 1897. But after initial success the old problem of a critical and anti-Semitic press reared its ugly head. In the cartoon (left) he is the monkey who must ride on the back of his superior as they leave the theatre.

Archiv für Kunst und Geschichte

Mahler's Sixth Symphony had its première in Vienna on 4 January 1907. The caricature (above) pokes fun at his use of unusual percussion instruments. 'Good God!' Mahler is supposed to be saying, 'Fancy leaving out the motor horn! Now I shall have to write another symphony!'

Bildarchiv Preussischer Kulturbesitz

Beautiful socialite Alma Schindler (above) met Mahler in the autumn of 1901. Her marriage, a few months later, to Vienna's most eligible bachelor was the talk of Viennese society (below).

This, plus a peaceful summer spent with Justine and Nathalie at Wörthersee, restored both his health and his creativity. He not only revised his Fourth Symphony, but wrote two huge movements of his Fifth, plus seven beautiful *Lieder,* five of which are to the poetry of Friedrich Rückert.

A new romance

Mahler's return to Vienna in the autumn was the start of another hectic round of rehearsals, production headaches and critical sniping. On top of this the Munich première of his Fourth Symphony was disastrous – and was cruelly labelled by the critics as sheer 'musical madness'. So it was a depressed and lonely man who, in late November 1901, went to a party being held by an acquaintance. And it was here that he met the beautiful, 23-year-old society beauty Alma Maria Schindler for whom he conceived a violent passion.

Within a matter of days he found his feelings being returned, and their whirlwind courtship had started. By late December they were both sure enough of their feelings to announce their official engagement. The news burst upon Vienna like a bombshell, for Mahler was the city's most famous bachelor, and he was fêted by his audience at the opera. Consumed with desire for each other, the pair became lovers in the new year, and Alma fell pregnant. The need for an early wedding gave Mahler concern over the future of his sister Justine, whom he still looked after. But happily, Justine took this opportunity to announce her own engagement to her long-time beau, the violinist Arnold Rosé. The two weddings took place one day apart, Gustav and Alma's on 9 March 1902, and Justine's the day after. One casualty of this sudden domestic revolution was Natalie Bauer-Lechner. There was a complete break between her and Mahler. She never married.

Mahler was now content as never before: working with his usual fanaticism in his post at the opera, writing during the summer at Maiernigg on Wörthersee, and leading a quiet, spartan existence at home in Vienna. The greatest event for the new couple in that first year was the birth of their first child, Maria Anna.

From the start she was doted on by her father, and this withdrawn, quiet child gave him more conversational pleasure than his social peers. This was not really surprising – since his marriage Mahler had become more and more anti-social, he rarely liked to entertain, and liked going out even less. His increasingly reclusive nature and the dictatorial regime he imposed on Alma was a great strain for her. He demanded absolute obedience and tact from her, especially when it came to his precious hours spent composing. This Alma gave him, just as Justine and Natalie had done before her, and as the whole Mahler family had done before that. But it wasn't easy for her; Alma was highly intelligent, had a large circle of friends, and had been creative in her own right before her marriage.

Österreichische Nationalbibliothek

Mahler adored his first daughter Maria Anna (with him above) and he never really recovered from the shock of her death at the age of four.

However, she was slowly able to introduce some of her friends into their small circle: the composer Arnold Schoenberg and the poet Gerhard Hauptmann, both brilliant men who eventually became very close to Mahler.

Archiv für Kunst und Geschichte

A creative period

In the summer of 1904, with Alma pregnant for a second time, Mahler completed work on his Sixth Symphony, a dark and tragic work, and his series of *Kindertotenlieder* (Songs on the Death of Children) based on poems by Friedrich Rückert. For a man of outward contentment, this music bore worrying

Gustav Klimt 'Salome'. Museo d'Arte Moderna, Venice/Bridgeman Art Library

indications of deep inner disturbance. Alma found it impossible to warm to the beautiful songs in the *Kindertotenlieder,* and felt that they were a dreadful temptation to fate. But time passed, the baby was born and all was well.

It was somehow fitting that Mahler's last complete year in Vienna, 1906, should have coincided with a series of performances celebrating the 150th anniversary of Mozart's birth. During the course of the year he gave new and brilliant productions of five great Mozart operas, all of them dear to his heart, as well as a special gala performance of *Cosi fan tutte* for the Royal Court in Salzburg.

He also had good reason to feel that, at long last, he had 'arrived' as a composer in the public eye. The past two years had seen increasing performances of his music all round Europe. But the time he needed to appear at these occasions became the direct cause of a split with the Vienna Opera in early 1907. His absences had led to bickering and unrest among the public and critics, and word was openly circulating in Vienna that the search was on for Mahler's successor. While this was not actually true, Mahler was tired of the constant battles, the excessive workload and the fickleness of his public. He tendered his resignation.

The year of 1907 was to prove decisive in ways that reached far beyond Mahler's work. That summer at Wörthersee, his younger daughter, Anna Justine, fell ill with scarlet fever. She recovered, only to pass on the infection to her sister Maria. But Maria contracted a secondary infection, failed to respond to treatment and, within days, was dead. Soon after this Alma's mother suffered a stroke. The strain of these two tragedies affected Alma's heart, and a doctor was called. He took the opportunity, while he was there, to check Mahler's heart, only to find that it was already diseased. The distraught couple had a new nightmare to contend with.

At the end of the year – having concluded a contract in New York at the Metropolitan Opera, for a huge salary and a shorter season than those in Vienna – Mahler made his farewell appearance in Vienna conducting *Fidelio.* It was a highly emotional occasion with a tearful audience giving 30 curtain-calls to the equally tearful Mahler.

The tempting of fate two years previously had borne bitter fruit and Mahler was a changed man. Death had been a constant presence in his family all his life: but the death of his daughter had the most devastating effect. He was forced to abandon all strenuous exercise – something he had always enjoyed – and live like a convalescent. This very nearly completely broke his spirit. From this time on, his priorities changed radically, as did his music.

The declining years

Mahler's time spent in New York, from his début at the Metropolitan on New Year's Day, 1908, at the age of 47, to his last performance in front of the New York Philharmonic in early 1911, was one of reduced vitality and an increased concentration on financial security and his later symphonies. He had a three-month commitment to an opera company with

Mahler was very keen to put on Richard Strauss's new opera* Salome *in Vienna. But the sensuous Salome (above) was considered too risqué for the opera ever to emerge from behind the ornate curtain of the Vienna Opera House (right). So Mahler had to be content to display his lively and progressive conducting (in silhouette below) on less controversial operas.

Archiv für Kunst und Geschichte

Bildarchiv Preussischer Kulturbesitz

Archiv für Kunst und Geschichte

Mahler made his last trip to America early in 1911 but his health failed and he was forced to return at the end of a month. The photograph (left) on his homeward journey was the last to be taken of him.

Archiv für Kunst und Geschichte

In August 1910, Mahler consulted Sigmund Freud (below left) to help sort out the marital and emotional difficulties which existed between him and Alma. From this meeting Mahler gained an understanding of these problems, as well as a deeper insight into his creative personality.

incomparable singers such as Caruso, but he had the misfortune of having a second-rate orchestra and the disadvantage of having to spend more time convalescing. Nevertheless the performances were brilliantly illuminated by his genius for two seasons, although he never gave his heart and soul to the New World. Always he longed to be back in Vienna, despite the incredible warmth the New Yorkers displayed.

It was back in Austria during the summers that he found the strength and inspiration to write his two heartfelt valedictory symphonies, *Das Lied von der Erde* and the Ninth. They were different from anything he had written before and, with the lack of the gigantic struggles which punctuated his earlier works before finding peace, showed signs that he had come to terms with mortality. He also made considerable progress with his Tenth Symphony but, like Beethoven and Schubert before him, felt he was doomed to complete only nine symphonies.

A last chance

In the summer of 1910, all Alma's years of self-sacrifice finally caught up with her: she exploded, telling Mahler she couldn't stand her life of isolation, total subjection to his will and increasing emotional coldness any longer. She demanded that he change. Luckily, he could see that she was right and acknowledged it. In August of that year he attended a private analytical session with Sigmund Freud.

During the session, Mahler felt he had made several great breakthroughs concerning his own mental state, and both men acknowledged that they found each other fascinating. Freud later commented: 'I had much opportunity to admire the capability for psychological understanding in this man of genius.'

This encounter resulted in a renewal of Mahler's love and passion for Alma. Before they made a return visit to New York in January 1911, Mahler made every effort to redress the years of unacknowledged sacrifice. The depth of his feeling is best shown in the dedication of the Tenth Symphony: 'To live for thee! To die for thee! Almschi!'

Unfortunately, this was the last opportunity he was to have, for within a short time of his starting the new season, Mahler's strength failed him. Within a month he was bedridden, rising only once to conduct a concert of music by his friend Ferruccio Busoni. It was to be his last. With his health now rapidly deteriorating, he and Alma returned to Europe.

Doctors in Paris confided to Alma that he had only a matter of weeks to live, perhaps just days. He was taken back to Vienna, frail and exhausted. Days after they arrived, on 18 May 1911, he died – a few weeks short of his 51st birthday.

On his death, Mahler finally received the adulation from the people of his beloved Vienna that had been denied to him all his life. As if beset by a deep sense of guilt at the way the composer had been vilified, Vienna gave him a funeral as impressive as any it had given its past musical heroes, and obituaries were unanimous in their expressions of profound loss. Mahler had finally won.

Mahler had started work on the score for his Tenth Symphony (a sample below) during the summer of 1909. But, as he had suspected, he was never to finish the work.

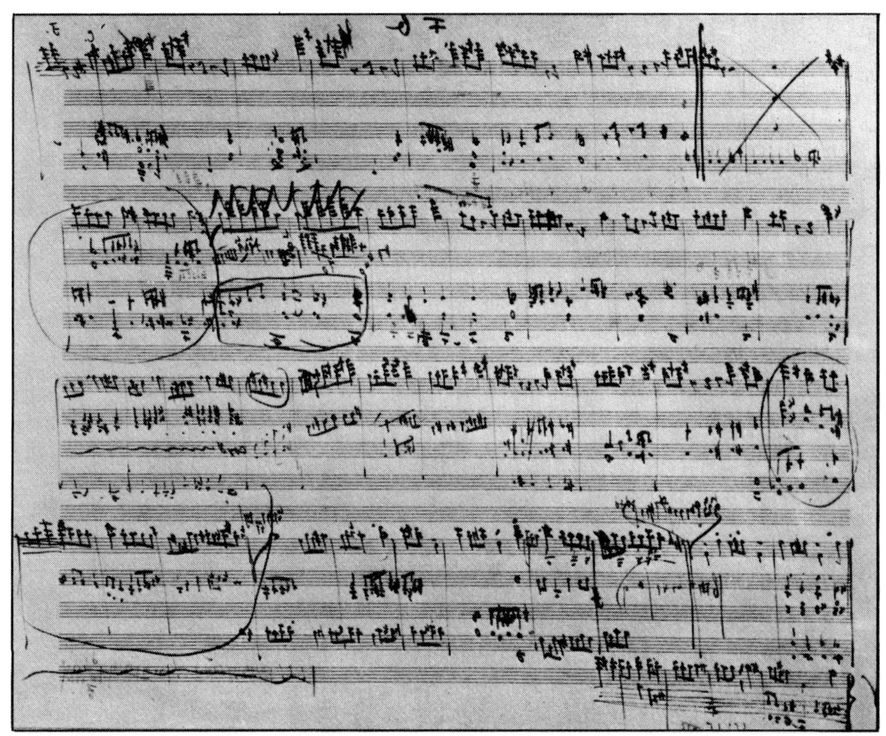

Private Collection

LISTENER'S GUIDE

The world of Mahler's symphonies

Chosen by Visconti for his film* Death in Venice, *Mahler's music is perhaps the ultimate expression of Romantic feeling and sensibility – the swansong of that visionary era.

As a composer Mahler lived in the world of the symphony, writing little else apart from song cycles – no concertos, no chamber music, no operas. 'The symphony is a world', he wrote. 'The symphony must embrace everything.'

To express that world view the composer, in Mahler's eyes, had to be a universal man, combining the talents of poet, painter, philosopher and musician in order to realize his vision. Mahler himself was no mean poet – often, in a spirit of fun, making up verses to Schubert's march melodies. As director of the Vienna opera he had plenty of scope to exercise his visual imagination in overseeing the stage setting and lighting effects, as well as directing the singers' movements. He read widely, particularly the philosophy of Kant and Goethe. And as a musician he brought all these gifts together in his choice of texts to set to music, the sensitivity with which he handled them and, above all, in his orchestral colouring – critics often talk of the range of colours in Mahler's palette.

The whole of creation

He wanted his music to express the whole of creation – the animal and human worlds – with a ladder leading up to heaven and its angels. His music is capable of expressing the most barren loneliness, the first stirrings of life, the wild abandonment of the Greek gods Dionysus and Pan in the midst of nature, and the anguish, self-doubt and tenderness of human feeling. Above all, it seems to convey man's longing for eternity or, as he wrote so expressively in the *Song of the Earth,* his desire to 'wander in the mountains' and see how 'everywhere and eternally the distance shines bright and blue. Eternally. Eternally'.

The outer world of nature and the inner world of man met in him so fruitfully due to his amazing and often self-torturing powers of introspection. In this respect he was a truly contemporary figure – the first great symphonist of the Freudian age. The composer Stockhausen, explaining why Mahler is such a key figure to the understanding of man, wrote: 'Should a higher being from a distant star wish to investigate the nature of Earthlings in a most concentrated moment, he could not afford to bypass Mahler's music.' It would help him understand man's range of passion 'from the most angelic to the most animal', the pain of his mortality, and his dreams of immortality.

Mahler's symphonies embrace a whole world of thought and feeling. They express man's deepest fears as well as his dreams of eternity – an eternity glimpsed amid the mountain peaks, where, in Mahler's words, 'everywhere and eternally the distance shines bright and blue' (left).

To express this range of emotion and experience, Mahler used the world of the orchestra in a way that no other composer, except perhaps Berlioz, had done before. He could descend to the depths with the darkest, muffled drums, muted brass, and plunging double basses; he could ascend the glistening peaks and the turrets of the Heavenly City with the brightest glockenspiel and most soaring woodwind. To achieve his effects he used enormous orchestral resources, with a great variety of percussion, often adding a Tam-Tam (oriental gong), guitar, mandolin, and cow bells – cow bells had a special significance for him, he explained, as they were the last terrestrial sound one hears before reaching the peak of a mountain. Contemporary reviewers, however, likened his use of the orchestra to the 'roaring of lions and the screaming of terrified sheep'. A cartoon in the humorous weekly *Die Muskete* showed an exasperated Mahler standing by a weird array of percussion instruments, including a hammer and vice, clutching his head in one hand, and a motor horn in the other, with the caption 'My God, I've forgotten the motor horn. Now I shall have to write another symphony!'

Light and shade

Mahler's use of the orchestra was, of course, conditioned by his experiences as a conductor. His scores contain very few *tutti* passages – where all the orchestra plays together – although when he wanted he could create a tremendous climax. Instead, they are full of beautiful solo passages, and contrasting groups of instruments playing against each other, as in the *Nachtmusik* of the Seventh Symphony. Despite the number of instruments used, all his efforts were directed to obtaining maximum clarity from the orchestra, with finely etched light and shade. Using the clearest part writing, he turns the players into a vast chamber orchestra, with one part moving pointedly against another.

Because Mahler saw the symphony as all-embracing, it had to include the experiences of everyday life too. That is why he brings in waltzes, marches, echoes of street musicians, birdsong, animal cries, bugle calls and tattoos from military barracks. Vocal movements exist side by side with instrumental ones; many of the words for these go back to childhood memories, and to a book of folk tales and poetry, rather like Grimm's *Fairy Tales,* called *Das Knaben Wunderhorn* (Youth's Magic Horn) that he had loved as a boy.

In these surrealistic poems, dead soldiers turn up on parade to answer roll call, girls entice sentries from their posts, St Anthony preaches a sermon to the fishes, and a nightingale and cuckoo hold a singing contest before a donkey judge. The book was closely associated in his mind with his early memories of living near an army barracks, with its constant bugle calls and marching bands. He learnt the folk tunes he uses to such good effect from Slavonic servant girls in his parents' employ, and was able to play them at the age of four on the accordion or concertina.

Deep affinity with nature

Mahler's life as a conductor was so hectic that he had to crowd all his composition into his summer holidays. As in the case of Brahms, the depths of the Austrian countryside proved a great source of inspiration. There he would swim and walk, composing in a hut built high up above the family house, furnished only with a piano, and volumes of Kant, Goethe, and the music of Bach.

The celebrated conductor Bruno Walter went to stay with Mahler shortly after the completion of the Third Symphony – two movements of which are described below. When Walter stopped to admire the magnificent scenery all around them, Mahler said: 'No need to look, I have composed all this already.' Walter was bowled over by the music:

The music made me feel I recognized him for the first time; his whole being seemed to breathe a mysterious affinity with the forces of nature . . . at the same time however – this in the last three movements – I was in contact with the longing of the human spirit to pass beyond its earthly and temporal bonds.

It took a long time for Mahler's music to be accepted. Its present popularity has been helped tremendously by the availability of stereo recordings which can do justice to his marvellous orchestration, and his place in the history of the symphony is now assured. He built on the programme elements in Beethoven's Sixth *(Pastoral)* and Ninth symphonies – the *Pastoral* has five movements – and followed Berlioz and Liszt in the development of programme music and proliferation of movements.

Symphony no. 5 in C sharp minor

3rd Movement: Adagietto. Sehr Langsam

In September 1910, after hearing a performance of Mahler's Eighth Symphony, the author Thomas Mann wrote to Mahler, enclosing one of his books as an acknowledgement of the pleasure the music had given him:

It is certainly a very poor return for what I received – a mere feather's weight in the hand of the man who, as I believe, expresses the art of our time in its profoundest and most sacred form.

Later, Mann was to base the character of Aschenbach on Mahler in his story *Death in Venice,* which tells how a lonely middle-aged writer is fascinated by the angelic beauty of the youth Tadzio, and follows him through the decaying streets of Venice, until his own death from cholera intervenes.

Programme notes

The Adagietto was the first piece of Mahler's music to become popular, and was often played at concerts on its own. It was also occasionally used as film music to express moments of romantic sorrow; but nowhere has it been used to better advantage than in Visconti's film *Death in Venice,* with its contrasting themes of beauty and decay. The movement is only some hundred bars long, a haven of peace between scherzo and finale, and is based on the setting Mahler wrote in 1904 of a poem written by Friedrich Rückert, which ends with the verse:

Ich bin gestorben dem Weltgetümmel und ruh' in einem stillen Gebiet! Iche leb' allein in meinem Himmel, in meinem Lieben, in meinem Lied.
(I am dead to the hurly burly of the world, and take my rest in a place of quietness. I am alone in my heaven, in my loving, in my song).

Fra Angelico 'Linaioli Altarpiece' (detail) San Marco, Florence/Scala

The radiant Adagietto of Mahler's Fifth Symphony, scored for harp and strings alone, calls to mind Fra Angelico's paintings of angels (centre).

It is celestial music, scored only for harp and strings. The harp does not seem so much an accompaniment as something that is happening on a higher plane than the more earthly strings, reminding one of those Italian paintings by Fra Angelico where angels with harps look fondly down from heaven at man's endeavours to reach their state. It lends itself perfectly to illustrating Mann's story about the dangerous allure of beauty for an artist trying to reach the spirit through the senses. The beautiful cannot be possessed in this world – it leads us on, as if from another, and we find it when we are 'dead to the world'.

The beautiful, halting melody is far from serene. If compared to the slow movement of Beethoven's Ninth Symphony, how tentative it seems, no sooner rising in ecstasy than falling back to earth to begin its climb again. The theme is at its calmest in its opening statement.

Example 1

It unfolds slowly, and then after a glowing passage which Mahler has marked *mit Warme* (with warmth), the yearning increases, and the violins climb falteringly higher and higher. The harp falls silent, watching their upward struggle, and then enters with a celestial chord, at which the violins collapse with an amazing sliding glissando, never to rise to such heights again. The harp plucks away, the theme limps along, and in the final bars harp and strings part ways.

Archiv für Kunst und Geschichte

The great German novelist, Thomas Mann (1875–1955 left), was deeply moved by Mahler's work, regarding it as the most serious and 'sacred' expression of the times. He based the central character of his masterpiece* Death in Venice *(1912) on the 'consumingly intensive personality' of Mahler, who had died in 1911. Later, Visconti, in his haunting film of the book, turned to Mahler's music for the soundtrack.

Rembrandt 'The Nightwatch'. Rijksmuseum-Stichting

Symphony no. 7 in E minor 'Song of the Night'

2nd Movement: Nachtmusik. Allegro moderato

This movement is the second of Mahler's Seventh symphony, which, with his Fifth and Sixth, forms a middle group of instrumental symphonies without choral reference or use of the *Wunderhorn* poems. Yet it carries us right back to that world of echoing bugle calls and shadows dancing in the light of a flickering fire or of the moon, where the trees stir in a whispering night wind.

Programme notes

Mahler called the movement *Nachtmusik* (Nocturne or Serenade), referring to it as a Night Patrol more or less in the manner of Rembrandt's famous painting, *The Night Watch*. It gives very much the feeling of a band of soldiers taking a stroll on a warm summer's night. Summoning and answering horns open a vast moonlit landscape between them. Then, such is the relaxation of tension, there seems to be almost a cessation of hostilities between two armies facing each other across a mythical border. Patrols can now stroll casually over a forbidden no-man's land.

After a magical opening, full of trills on the woodwind and abortive marches elsewhere, with Mahler frantically writing in the score *Nicht eilen!* (Don't hurry!) the 'stroll' gets under way on the horn.

Example 2

horn

pp

pp

This is one of the most relaxed, open-necked, loose-sleeved themes in all music. Mahler's use of the military march is here deeply ironic. The purposeful sense of

The echoing horn calls, muffled drum rolls and strange night whispers that reverberate across the night landscape of Mahler's* Nachtmusik 2 *suggest a night patrol setting out, very much in the manner of Rembrandt's* Night Watch *(above).

The fourth movement of Mahler's Third Symphony describes the awakening of man and is reminiscent of Michelangelo's Sistine fresco (right), where God wakes a sleeping Adam.

getting somewhere, whether with the march of an army, or of progress, or of time, is here slowed to a stroll. It is a march that gets nowhere, ending up a mountainside with cow bells sounding all around. Compared with the martial themes of Beethoven's Fifth Symphony marching confidently to victory, here, in the knowledge that no victory is possible, small bands of mercenaries – stragglers – reluctantly but happily pick up their packs and go for a stroll in an unfamiliar moonlit landscape. Nationalities, frontiers, ideologies are confused. It is an army without a leader, as bewildered as Bottom and his friends in *A Midsummer Night's Dream,* dispersing over the countryside after the crash of empires. Mahler's irony here makes him a true modern, a debunker of outmoded heroics.

The lack of a specific programme or text to illustrate has here helped Mahler to achieve some of his most fantastic orchestral effects. Pizzicato strings are set against trilling clarinets, as the stroll takes us into a Trio section. A theme on the cellos is punctuated by staccato horn burbles, and trills on triangle. Rolls on drum and gong add to the unearthly effect, where cellos tread warily with deliberate footsteps. The theme returns on horns barely audible among the cow bells, and then accompanied by swirling woodwind. The delights that follow are too numerous to mention, as Mahler piles on surprise after surprise, swinging his themes from piccolo to cello, with the the orchestra playing full, individual roles in between.

The end is magical, as the music descends through a mist of trills, arpeggios on the clarinet, and a final dying pizzicato on violins and cellos that seems to leave nothing else to say. But a last note high up above these is heard on harp and clarinet, looking back and forward at the same time.

Michelangelo 'The Creation of Adam' (detail). Sistine Chapel, Vatican, Rome/Scala

Understanding music: film music

The more popular music of long-dead composers has been plundered for films ever since the first movie projector rattled into action. Until the advent of sound in the 1920s, nearly all silent films were accompanied by live music – anything from a pianist to a full orchestra – fitting the action on the screen as best as possible.

Some film distributors provided cue sheets prescribing recommended sequences of mood music which would include excerpts from Beethoven (used for accompanying dog fights in the air), 'chase music' popularly represented by Rossini's *William Tell* Overture, and Massenet's *Elégie* from *Thaïs* to console 'sadness', while *The Swan* from Saint-Saën's *The Carnival of Animals* provided a suitable romantic atmosphere and a new dimension to the term, 'programme music'. Though original music was also written in the form of short descriptive pieces entitled *Help! Help!* or *Broken Vows,* a few more 'serious' composers wrote especially tailored scores – one of Shostakovich's earliest forays into the genre was the music to accompany the silent epic, *New Babylon.*

Sound film brought a new challenge. Composers were now expected to cue musical gestures to the split second. An intricate system has since evolved which basically involves the composer fitting his score to a detailed time sheet of the action. The music is converted to metronome markings (the number of beats per minute) which in turn are recorded as 'clicks' or electronic impulses, on the frames of the film. The 'clicks-track' is then played back to the conductor through earphones as he conducts the music while watching the action projected on a screen behind the orchestra. This technical challenge, however, inspired a growing number of highly proficient film-music composers. Max Steiner, for example, who wrote the music for *Gone with the Wind* (among nearly 300 other film scores) and Dmitri Tiomkin (*High Noon,* where the score was especially composed round the song *Do not forsake me, O my darling*), created orchestral scores which vie with the great Romantic composers in brilliance and panache. However, music from the 'classical' repertoire continues to be borrowed with varying degrees of success. Kubrick's use of Johann Strauss's *Blue Danube* waltz in his film *2001 – A Space Oddysey* is both witty and enhancing, but in Disney's *Fantasia,* where animated deer court to Beethoven's *Pastoral* Symphony, the adaptation is perhaps of more questionable taste. On the whole though, animated films have a commendable record of a highly apt use for music, both original and 'classical'. This is cleverly illustrated by Scott Bradley's cunning and witty musical puns in the *Tom and Jerry* cartoons, and even the most ardent Wagner fan would find it hard to be offended by Bugs Bunny's rendering of *The Ring.*

The contribution of such major 20th-century composers as Prokofiev, Walton and Copland, though relatively incidental to their main work is, however, fascinating, since they bring to the craft a fresh perspective. In the opinion of the great Russian film director, Eisenstein, Prokofiev's music for his film *Alexander Nevsky* achieved a unique synthesis between sound and image through precise matching of aural and visual rhythms. Walton's music for *Henry V* again succeeds thanks to the close collaboration and mutual respect between the composer and the director, Laurence Olivier – an infrequent instance in the fast, commercially pressured world of the cinema. Aaron Copland, meanwhile, won an Academy Award in 1949 for his music to *The Heiress,* which starred Olivia de Haviland.

Even now, the work of many great composers, such as Mahler, Albinoni and even Mozart, is known to the public at large only because a film director has used it to create the right mood for a film.

***In* Death in Venice, *Visconti converted Mann's Aschenbach from an author to a composer who, inspired by the beauty of the boy Tadzio (below), composes the music for* 'O Mensch! Gib Acht!'**

The Kobal Collection

Piero della Francesca 'The Nativity' (detail). The National Gallery, London/Edimedia

Symphony no. 3 in D minor 'A Summer Morning's Dream'

If the nocturnal movements of the Seventh Symphony are Mahler's Midsummer Night's Dream, the Third Symphony is his Midsummer Morning's Dream.

Although he never published a programme for this Symphony, thinking that it might detract from the music, Mahler did in fact work to one, calling it at one time *The Joyful Science. A Summer Morning's Dream* in six, originally seven, movements:

1 Summer marches in.
2 What the flowers of the meadow tell me.
3 What the beasts of the forest tell me.
4 What the night tells me (of man).
5 What the morning bells tell me (of angels).
6 What love tells me.

The fourth and fifth movements are described below.

Programme notes

4th Movement: 'O Mensch, Gib Acht!' ('O man, pay heed!') Sehr langsam. Misterioso

In this movement, an Adagio setting of Nietsche's *Midnight Song* for contralto, man awakens from his creation to find that he is the only creature that longs for eternity.

Marked *sehr langsam, misterioso* (very slowly, mysteriously), it opens with an eerie theme on cellos and double basses.

O Mensch! (O man!), sings the contralto. *Gib Acht!* (Take heed!) And then, before the repetition of *Gib Acht!* Mahler opens up a vast space, with harps and trombones providing a pinpoint of light in the darkness. The contralto continues:

Was spricht die tiefe Mitternacht?/Ich schlief! Aus tiefem Traum bin ich erwacht!/Die Welt ist tief!/Und tiefer, als der Tag gedacht!
(What does the deep midnight say? I was asleep, from deep dreams I have awoken. The world is deep, and deeper than the day imagined!)

A violin sends a ray of light, and an oboe gives the call of a bird in the loneliness, creating a wonderful feeling of dawn. The repetition of the words *O Mensch,* added by Mahler to the poem, is now brighter, as the prospect of the joys and sorrows of this life hold a promise of eternity:

Tief ist ihr Weh!/Lust, tiefer noch als Herzeleid!/Weh spricht: Vergeh!/Doch alle Lust will Ewigkeit!/Will tiefe, tiefe Ewigkeit.
(Deep is its grief! Joy, deeper still than heartache! Grief says: Die! But all joy seeks eternity. Seeks deep, deep eternity.)

After the radiance shed on the orchestration by this glimpse of eternity, the orchestra sinks back into darkness.

***Bimm bamm** sing the choir of angels (above) in Mahler's Third Symphony, accompanied by the joyous peal of morning bells.*

5th Movement: 'Bimm bamm. Es sangen drei Engel einen süssen Gesang' ('Bimm bamm, three angels in sweet harmony sang')

But now, out of the darkness, amid the joyful bell peals, comes the brightness of a choir of boy angels singing of the bliss of heaven.

Example 3

Bimm bamm bimm bamm

Bimm bamm, they sing, imitating the ringing of bells, their lips humming out the final 'm's as Mahler requested in the score. The women's chorus joins in the celebrations with the story of the three angels:

Es sangen drei Engel einen süssen Gesang:/Mit Freuden es selig in dem Himmel klang,/Sie jauchzen fröhlich auch dabei,/Das Petrus sei von Sünden frei.
(Three angels were singing a sweet song./In blissful joy it rang through heaven./They shouted too for joy,/That Peter was set free from sin.)

The movement is only 128 bars long, and the *Bimm Bamms* run through nearly its whole length, only stopping for the troubled middle section. Here strings are used for the first time to shadow the brightness of wind, horns, harps, and glockenspiel, as the contralto sings Peter's answer to Jesus' question: 'Why do you stand here? When I look at you, you weep at me.'

Und sollt' ich nich weinen du gütiger Gott?/Ich hab übertreten die zehn Gebot./ Ich gehe and weine ja bitterlich./Ach komm' und erbärme dich über mich!
(And should I not weep, thou bounteous God? I have broken the ten commandments. I wander weeping bitterly,/O come and have mercy on me!)

Happily, forgiveness is at hand, and the angels can *Bimm bamm* away happily from their heavenly belfries.

Die himmlische Freud' ist eine selige Stadt./Die himmlische Freud'die kein Ende mehr hat!/Die himmlische Freude war Petro bereit't./Durch Jesum, und allen zur Seligkeit.
(Heavenly joy is a blessed city. Heavenly joy that has no end! Heavenly joy was granted to Peter, Through Jesus, and to all men for eternal bliss.)

With this joyful affirmation, the ringing voices of the choir and the bright fanfares of brass recede into the distance and the movement draws to a close. This is music which, to use Mahler's own words, expresses 'the highest ecstasy of the most joyous zest for living' as opposed to 'the most burning desire for death.

Symphony no. 1 in D major ('The Titan')

2nd Movement:
Kräftig bewegt, doch nicht zu schnell
Mahler's first symphony was begun in 1884 in Kassel, completed in 1888 at Leipzig, and premièred in Budapest in 1889. When it was performed in June 1894 at a music festival in Weimar, it was roundly denounced by the critics as a crime against the law and order of symphonic music. The outcry was largely directed at the bitter sarcasm of the slow movement, a grotesque funeral march to the tune of Frère Jacques, although the composer's innovation in using seven horns was seen as unnecessary self-indulgence.

It was written at a time of high emotion in Mahler's life. In 1886, he had fallen passionately in love with a much older woman, the wife of Weber's grandson, and the relationship had come to a tragic end, to which he gave expression in the symphony. Bruno Walter has described the work as Mahler's *Werther,* comparing it with Goethe's first novel *Werther's Leiden* (The sorrows of young Werther).

But it was another novel which, in fact, inspired Mahler's First Symphony – a work by the German poet Jean Paul Richter called *The Titan,* a title which Mahler originally used for his symphony, and by which it has since been known.

Programme notes

Mahler laid out a full programme for the work; part one – 'From the days of youth, youth-fruit-and-thorn pieces' – is full of optimism and the joys of youth. The movement on this record – a Waltz-Scherzo – concludes the happy first half of the symphony, and was given the description 'Full Sail'.

The movement opens with a heavy stamping figure in the bass. Then comes a simple Moravian folk dance melody which Mahler uses to bring off wonderful effects of light and shade, and contrasts of texture. The form is that of the classical minuet and trio, but within it Mahler displays a technique of orchestration and variety of pace that were years ahead of his time. The strict, rhythmic dance figure allows him to indulge in some exuberant part writing, particularly for horns and trumpets.

The lovely floating theme of the trio leads to another Waltz, but this time a much schmalzier and urbane version, as if some fashionable Viennese on a country outing had decided to join in. Then the peasants take the floor – or the field – again to round the movement off on an exuberant note. But, to place the movement in its Mahlerian context, it must be remembered that the descending fourths of the dance rhythm are soon to become the plodding feet of the funeral march which follows in the next movement.

Great interpreters

Rafael Kubelik (conductor)
Born in Czechoslovakia in 1914, Kubelik studied both composition and conducting at Prague Conservatory, making his début with the Czech Philharmonic Orchestra in 1934. He became acting conductor of the orchestra in 1936, and in 1937 brought the orchestra to Belgium and England. From 1939–41 he was conductor at the Brno National Theatre before returning to the Philharmonic, this time as artistic director. He stayed in this position throughout the War, often running directly counter to the German occupational forces' wishes, leaving only in 1948 when the communist government came to power.

Stopping briefly in England, Kubelik finally settled in Switzerland before developing his new career, dividing his commitments between the US and Europe. He was appointed musical director of the Chicago Symphony Orchestra in 1950, running into controversy regularly for his programmes. He resigned finally in 1953, taking up guest appearances on the concert stage for most of the rest of the 1950s. He became music director at Covent Garden in 1955, and had some notable successes there, including *Les Troyens, Jenufa* and *Die Meistersinger.* But, in the wake of public criticism from Sir Thomas Beecham, which hurt him deeply, he reluctantly resigned.

In 1961 he began his long association with the Bavarian Radio Symphony Orchestra. It has been with this orchestra that most of his memorable recorded performances have been made. Pride of place here goes to the Mahler symphony cycle, and to the première recording of Pfitzner's remarkable opera, *Palestrina.*

Death in Venice
Luchino Visconti's film *Death in Venice,* starring Dirk Bogarde, was based on the book by Thomas Mann, itself inspired by Mahler's life and music. Appropriately, the film used famous excerpts from Mahler's music, all of which have been discussed here, to emphasize the fatal atmosphere of Venice in 1911.

FURTHER LISTENING

Mahler symphonies and lieder

Symphony no. 9 in D (1909)
Each Mahler symphony has something special to recommend it and make it unique. This, the last numbered symphony he completed before his death, is unique in its burning, heartfelt lyricism and its pervading sense of valedictory resignation. A massive work on a huge scale, its first movement, the *Andante comodo* which lasts all of 25 minutes, is full of foreboding, tension and outbursts of affirmation.

Symphony no. 2
In the vast, all-embracing scheme of this work, subtitled the 'Resurrection', Mahler found his true musical voice. It is a work with a gigantic musical superstructure as well as a complete philosophical programme which the music is intended to elucidate. Whether one chooses to follow this or not, the sheer power and force of the work is undeniable, and the moments of stillness and reflection, such as the song *Urlicht,* are all the more precious for being so hard-won.

Rückert-Lieder (1902)
Whereas the symphonies display the full range of Mahler's ideas and emotions, and are therefore often stormy and chaotic, his orchestral lieder show more exclusively the lyrical side of his nature. The five songs that go to make up Mahler's settings of poems by the German orientalist poet Friedrich Rückert have more than a passing affinity with the sublime music of the Adagietto from his Fifth Symphony – not surprisingly as they were almost contemporaneous.

IN THE BACKGROUND

'Finished'

In 1900 Vienna was the cosmopolitan capital of the doomed Hapsburg Empire. Haunted by a sense of living on borrowed time, its anxious citizens found a refuge in art and music.

A typical street scene in turn-of-the-century Vienna (above). At the point where the tree-lined Ringstrasse meets Kärntnerstrasse, with the Opera House in the background, Viennese stroll, meet and gossip.

In 1900 Vienna was the capital of a huge, disintegrating empire. The forces of nationalism had been eating away at Austria-Hungary throughout the 19th century. To the south, the Italians had thrown Austrian troops out of Lombardy and Venice. To the north, Prussia had decisively ejected Austria from the sphere of German politics. Meanwhile, the Slavs, Czechs and Hungarians were clamouring for their own national parliaments – leaving the crisis-ridden administration in Vienna paralysed. The imposing two-headed eagle on the emperor's coat of arms symbolized the dual monarchy of Austria-Hungary, but to many it became a reminder of the ludicrous complexity of the Hapsburg civil service: how could a two-headed creature successfully govern such a vast and unwieldy state?

The Mayerling affair

Despite the nationalist ferments tearing at the empire's fabric during the 19th century, Vienna's liberal middle class had remained optimistic until two shocking crises permanently eroded morale. Wealthy, professional citizens (many of whom were Jewish) hoped that education, industrialization and the extension of voting rights would make their chaotic motherland evolve into a modern, multinational and democratic state. But their faith in the economic future was shaken by the stock market crash of 1873, which became known as Black Friday, and a further blow came in 1889 with the shocking 'Mayerling affair'.

On 29 January 1889 the young heir to the throne, Crown Prince Rudolph, shot himself at his hunting lodge in the Vienna Woods and also killed his 17-year-old lover, Marie Vetsera. A hasty and inept attempt to pretend that he had died of heart failure was dropped when the old emperor, Franz Joseph, insisted on publishing the basic details of the whole tragic story. As the circumstances surrounding the Mayerling affair became public knowledge it became clear that, far from having been an able, humane and liberal young man, Rudolph had been very unsound mentally and he had lived in a world of sexual chaos.

The Mayerling affair was the last straw. Many Austrians had hoped that Rudolph's accession to the throne would bring a new vitality to the ailing empire, but now there was nothing to hope for. From this point on, they regarded the ageing Franz Joseph as the end of his line. After him, there would be nothing. The new heir to the throne, Archduke Franz Ferdinand, was widely distrusted. It was his assassination at Sarajevo that finally drove Austria over the abyss into the First World War, and yet there was little sorrow expressed at his death. On the afternoon of his murder, a hot Sunday in June 1914, a mild middle-of-the-road politician named Josef Redlich recorded the event in his diary. His entry concluded with the thought that perhaps God had

BPCC/Aldus Archive

Emperor Franz Joseph mixed only with members of the huge imperial family. Court occasions (left) were usually restricted to the blue-blooded nobility, the diplomatic corps and officers on active service in Vienna. The 'Old Gentleman', as Franz Joseph was called, disapproved of Karl Lueger (below), the brilliantly opportunist politician who was mayor of Vienna from 1897 to 1910.

In 1889 all Vienna was scandalized when Crown Prince Rudolf (bottom), heir to the throne, shot himself and his teenage lover, Marie Vetsera (bottom left), at Mayerling.

Bildarchiv Preussischer Kulturbesitz

been kind to the Austrians in sparing them an emperor who was said to possess 'the callousness and cruelty of an Asian despot'.

The death of liberalism

In France, the rise of the middle classes had destroyed the power of the court, and in Britain wealthy industrialists had married into the aristocracy to create a new alliance between traditional privilege and commercial wealth. But in Vienna this alliance failed. Through the complexities of official protocol, the court remained closed to the rising world of bourgeois power. In order to be presented at court, you had to trace your noble ancestry back through 11 generations. One wealthy American visitor to Vienna, Consuelo Vanderbilt, thought the hereditary rulers of Austria resembled an over-bred species of pedigree dog: 'The aristocratic Austrians I met looked like greyhounds with their long, lean bodies and small heads. It was, I thought, a pity that they could express their thoughts in so many languages, when they had so few thoughts to express.'

But despite the fact that the court establishment left them out in the cold, Vienna's middle class felt compelled to support the old regime, simply because what was threatening to succeed it was far more frightening. The working class was turning to socialism and to virulent strains of German nationalism, which were heavily tinged with anti-Semitism.

Archiv für Kunst und Geschichte

Hans Makart. Historisches Museum der Stadt Wien/Mick Gold Archiv

For the emperor's silver wedding celebrations in 1879 Hans Makart, the 'wizard' of the Ringstrasse era, organized a historical pageant (above). Dressed in a Rubens costume and mounted on a white charger, Makart himself rode at the head of the procession, which marched round the Ringstrasse.

Edimages

After the demolition of the old city walls in the 1850s, the Ringstrasse (right), which girdled the inner city, became Vienna's principal thoroughfare.

Gustav Klimt, the leading painter of Mahler's day, had to free himself of Hans Makart's influence before he could establish his own distinctive style. Makart's sensuous ladies (below) loll in a typically cluttered and rich setting, but Klimt's client (right), the daughter of a rich Secession patron, is depicted with photographic realism against a stylized background.

Georg von Schönerer had organized the radical German nationalists in the 1880s and led them into extreme anti-Semitic politics. He never succeeded in forming a powerful party but he elevated anti-Semitism into a major disruptive force in Austrian politics. But Schönerer's political techniques influenced Karl Lueger, who did succeed in mobilizing the lower middle class as a political force, and he transformed this movement into the Christian Socialists in the 1890s. A skilled operator and a powerful leader, Lueger became the hero of the ordinary men and women of Vienna, who idolized him as *der schöne Karl* (handsome Karl) – the sworn enemy of financial speculators and Jewish bankers.

Three times Lueger was elected Mayor of Vienna before Franz Joseph (who deplored any trace of anti-Semitism) agreed to ratify his appointment. Eventually the emperor capitulated and from 1897 until his death in 1910, handsome Karl ruled over his beloved city. Although he was quick to denounce Jewish financiers for controlling the economy, he also included Jewish bankers among his supporters and advisers. When questioned about this contradiction, Lueger replied, 'I decide who is a Jew and who isn't.'

With the rise of Lueger, Vienna's wealthy middle class, who had once believed in progress and universal suffrage, found themselves propping up a moribund aristocracy while fearing the politics of the mob. More and more, this alienated middle class withdrew into the world of culture. They cultivated artists and musicians as heroes and saw in the realm of art an asylum from a hopeless present and a terrifying future.

Behind the façade

Vienna had been dramatically modernized in the second half of the 19th century. In 1857 Franz Joseph had ordered the medieval walls to be demolished and replaced by a great, circular road – the Ringstrasse – adorned with parks and lavish public buildings. By the time it was completed, in the 1880s, the Ringstrasse had become the showplace of liberal values, dominated by buildings that symbolized the modern secular state: parliament, university, art gallery and town hall. Historicism was the architectural style – a style that borrowed the most appropriate look from the history book. So the parliament looked like a Greek temple; the town hall looked suitably Gothic; and the opera house looked like a Venetian palace.

The leading artist of the Ringstrasse era was Hans Makart and he was a genius at historicism. He painted vast canvases overflowing with gorgeous costumes

and exotic props, and at his studio he and his friends loved to hold parties in historical fancy dress. Makart was the art director of the Ringstrasse era and the entire city of Vienna was stage managed by his elaborate designs.

For the modern artists who grew up in the late 19th century, the Ringstrasse came to epitomize everything they loathed about Vienna: it was phoney, it was pretentious, it was living in the past. 'We are the working people of today. We should be ashamed to live in the style of princes and patricians of yesterday. We are not the Baroque age, we don't live in the Renaissance. Why should we act as if we did?' wrote the critic Hermann Bahr.

A young architect, Adolf Loos, went even further. In his hard-hitting essay, *Ornament and Crime,* he argued that meaningless ornamentation was a form of degeneracy. Loos succeeded in designing one building in the centre of Vienna that was so free of ornamentation that he shocked the public, the critics and even the emperor. It was situated on the Michaelerplatz (opposite an entrance to the Hofburg, the imperial palace) and it had a simple

Hans Makart 'Marmorherzen'. Bildarchiv Preussischer Kulturbesitz

Gustav Klimt 'Margarethe Stonborough-Wittgenstein'. Neue Pinakothek, Munich/Joachim Blauel-Artothek

Österreichische Nationalbibliothek

Members of the Vienna Secession at the Beethoven Exhibition of 1902 (above) – their first president, Gustav Klimt, is seated in the armchair. This, the 14th Secession Exhibition, was based on Max Klinger's statue of Beethoven. The poster (right) was designed by Alfred Roller, who made his name as stage designer for Gustav Makart at the opera.

façade. Legend has it that Franz Joseph described this building as 'the house without eyebrows' and, having seen it once, he refused to use that entrance to his palace again.

The Secession

It was precisely this feeling of being smothered by the past that prompted Vienna's young artists to organize the Secession movement in 1898. They were aware of artistic developments abroad and they wanted to create an exhibition space and a public forum for modern art in Vienna. But it all began as a very polite form of artistic rebellion and the first president of the Secession movement, Gustav Klimt, invited Franz Joseph to open their first exhibition.

As a student Klimt had worked in Makart's studio and it was widely believed that he would be the heir to Makart's artistic empire. Through the 1890s Klimt continued to work successfully in the historicist tradition, painting frescoes for the Burgtheater and the Art Museum. But just as Klimt was confirming his role as Vienna's leading artist by initiating the Secession movement, an extraordinary scandal erupted around his latest Ringstrasse project.

He had been commissioned to paint frescoes representing justice, philosophy and medicine for the University of Vienna, but when the public and the critics took their first look at this work in progress, there was a storm of protest. Klimt had broken away from the style of Makart's historical pageants and created something much more disturbing. His image of philosophy showed a writhing column of naked people ascending one side of the picture, while on the other side a sphynx-like face peered through the clouds. What upset people most, however, was that the image seemed extremely pessimistic. 'This picture shows how humanity is no more than a dull mass, which in the eternal service of procreation is driven hither and thither, as if in a dream, from joy to sorrow, from the first stirrings of life to powerless collapse into the grave', said one newspaper.

The university scandal

Klimt was so angered by the public and political attack on his work that he altered the painting of

Alfred Roller 'Poster for the 14th Exhibition of the Secession', Historisches Museum der Stadt Wien

jurisprudence that he was engaged on, to make it even more sinister. Klimt's image of justice showed a naked man arraigned in front of three predatory women, who resembled the Furies of Greek mythology, while a gigantic squid wrapped its tentacles around the wretched sinner. Eighty-seven faculty members signed a petition denouncing the work. After an outcry lasting five years, Klimt repaid the fee he had received from the Ministry of Culture, and the works were then bought by wealthy private collectors. By handing back his commission, Klimt was acknowledging that he could no longer work

Bildarchiv Preussischer Kulturbesitz

A house designed by Adolf Loos was a plain, geometric structure (left). Rebelling against ornamentation of any kind, this radical architect gave modern architecture a new, simple beauty. The Secessionists, like Loos, were fighting against the stifling historicism of contemporary Viennese art. But even the simple ornamentation of this interior (below left) – designed by the Secessionist Otto Wagner – offended Loos's dictum that architecture should display a functional simplicity of form.

with the state on this kind of public statement.

In the event, the scandal of the University paintings did not have a devastating effect on Klimt's career. Although he no longer received official commissions from the City Council, there were plenty of private patrons who were interested in his work. He was now sought out by the cultivated middle class, a clientele with a strong Jewish element – hostile critics sometimes attacked Klimt's work as 'Jewish taste'. In his portraits of the artistically inclined wives of Viennese industrialists, he was able to carry out some of his most daring pictorial experiments.

Klimt would set a face rendered with photographic realism against elaborately stylized surroundings that combined Byzantine mosaics, Cretan wall paintings and oriental metal work. The dramatic interplay between Klimt's highly naturalistic manner of portraying faces and the artificial environments in which he placed them gave his work its particular distinction. In addition, the central thematic obsessions of his art – eroticism, cycles of life, generation and death, and female power and sexuality – mirror quite accurately the concerns of intellectuals in Vienna at the turn of the century, showing the artist to have been entirely in tune with his times.

While Klimt and the artists of the Secession movement were producing elegant forms of modern art to the Secessionist motto, 'To each time, its own art: to that art its own freedom' Gustav Mahler was writing his epic symphonies and struggling to modernize the style of the Viennese opera. The architects Otto Wagner, Josef Hoffmann, Joseph Maria Olbrich and Adolf Loos were breaking from classicism, designing landmark buildings which did much to advance the Modernist style. Meanwhile, Arnold Schoenberg and his pupils Alban Berg and Anton von Webern were beginning to compose atonal music, and the playwright Arthur Schnitzler and novelist Robert Musil were writing about a city that was troubled by identity problems. The affluent ladies who sat for Klimt also attended Mahler's operas, and when they were feeling anxious they could visit Sigmund Freud, who pioneered psychoanalysis in their city.

Twilight in Vienna

In its last 20 years as an imperial capital (before the outbreak of the First World War in 1914 brought about the long-awaited disintegration of Austria-Hungary) Vienna produced an extraordinary flowering of innovative talent. And partly because of their shared sense of alienation, there was a great deal of collaboration between artists of all kinds.

The Secessionists hoped to achieve their aims of introducing the Viennese public to new art and bringing the city's artists into contact with the latest international trends through exhibitions. The first exhibition in 1898 was a tremendous success. Perhaps most impressive was the mixed character of the exhibition, which featured not only paintings but also graphics, sculpture, architectural designs and objects of applied art.

For their 1902 exhibition, they combined music and architecture in order to honour a statue of Beethoven which had been made by a German sculptor Max Klinger. They designed an elaborate pavilion for the statue and created a succession of murals and sculptures to lead the viewer into Beethoven's presence. Mahler arranged part of Beethoven's ninth symphony for a brass ensemble and conducted them at the opening ceremony. In the magnificent Beethoven frieze, which Klimt painted for this exhibition, there was a figure of a knight in armour that seemed to resemble Gustav Mahler. Certainly, Mahler and Klimt respected each other for they had both achieved the same dubious honour. Both men had risen to the highest artistic status and then found themselves denounced by newspapers and governments.

Angelo Hornak

It was a common fate for Viennese intellectuals. 'Gustav Klimt is truly Viennese. One can see that from his pictures, but also from the fact that he is honoured throughout the world and attacked only in Vienna', wrote Felix Salten. When Loos published his book about the connections between architecture and morality, he gave it the title *Ins Leere Gesprochen* (Spoken into the Void) to convey his view that no one in Vienna was listening. And indeed many of Vienna's most radical thinkers felt compelled to leave the city that either ignored or vilified them. At the turn of the century Vienna had seen a brilliant concentration of talent in music and the arts, but gradually the artists withdrew into a private world, like Klimt, or simply left for other places. By 1914 many were gone from Vienna.

When Mahler left Vienna for America a small group of friends accompanied him to the station to bid him farewell. As the train steamed away into the distance, it was Gustav Klimt who uttered the word which hung over this group of artists and their audience: 'Finished!'

Contemporary composers

Georges Bizet (1838-75)

Bizet was an infant prodigy, being sent to the Paris Conservatoire at the age of 10 to study under Gounod and Halévy. At 17 he wrote the *Symphony in C* – now a concert repertory piece – and won the Prix de Rome for his operetta *Le Docteur Miracle*. Back in Paris, his opera *Les Pêcheurs de Perles* was savaged by the critics when staged in 1863. Upset by this reaction, he wrote little until the exquisite *L'Arlesienne* suite of 1872, which shows the first signs of his mature style. By then he was already working on his masterpiece, *Carmen,* which opened in 1875 at the Opéra-Comique. The audience remained indifferent, the press found it scandalous, for it was the first *opéra comique* (with spoken dialogue) to portray an anti-heroine. Bizet died on the day of its 31st performance, convinced of his opera's failure. It is now perhaps the most popular of all operas.

Max Bruch (1838-1920)

Born in Cologne, Bruch studied there and at Bonn, teaching before he became *Kapellmeister* to the Prince of Schwarzburg-Sondershausen in 1867. Later he held various conducting posts, including three years at Liverpool (1880–83), then he became teacher of composition at Berlin Hofschule (1892–1910). His works include operas, an operetta, choral works (much admired in Germany) and orchestral works in the Mendelssohn-Spohr style. Of these the most famous is his *First Violin Concerto in G minor,* which is most notable for its extremely beautiful slow movement.

Anton Bruckner (1824-96)

Born in Ansfelden, Austria, the son of a village schoolmaster, Bruckner became a chorister at St Florian monastery, where he was made organist in 1848. In 1855 he moved to Vienna to study under Sechter at the Conservatory, finally succeeding his teacher in 1868. By then he had fallen under the spell of Wagner and composed two symphonies, one unnumbered. From this time dates his great *Mass in F minor* and two more symphonies, all attacked for their Wagnerian influences. As an organist, his fame spread abroad and he made several successful tours, gaining important pupils. His later symphonies – he wrote nine in all – were often cut by friends, which caused much controversy. In his last years his religious feelings, which permeate his work, grew ever stronger and he wrote little.

Edward MacDowell (1861-1908)

Born in New York, MacDowell studied there and in Paris, before moving to Germany where Liszt encouraged him to compose. In 1886 he returned to the United States, where he struggled to find time and energy to compose while working as a teacher or performer. His two orchestral suites, some piano pieces and public performances won him the first professorship of music at Colombia University in 1896, but he had to resign in 1904. Soon afterwards he showed signs of mental collapse and spent the rest of his life completely insane. His most typical works are those for piano, among them the *Woodland Sketches.*

Giacomo Puccini (1858-1924)

Born into a very musical family in Lucca, central Italy, he studied at the Milan Conservatory, where he was a pupil of Ponchielli. Under Verdi's influence, he decided to concentrate on opera, but his first attempt, *Le Villi,* was rejected because of its illegibility in 1883. Success only came with *Manon Lescaut* in 1893, for Puccini was a slow, if meticulous, composer. *La Bohème* (1896), *Tosca* (1900) and *Madam Butterfly* (1904), followed and have all become world favourites, though the last had a bad initial reception. Later operas, like *La Fanciulla del West,* premièred in New York in 1910, were less popular and his last work, *Turandot,* was unfinished when he died in Brussels.

Hugo Wolf (1860-1903)

Born in Windischarzm, Styria (now in Yugoslavia), Wolf was first taught by his father, before entering the Vienna Conservatory in 1875. This he had to leave for disciplinary reasons and for some years he made a precarious living teaching and writing for the *Wiener Salonblatt.* He made no secret of his fanatical pro-Wagner and anti-Brahms views, which did not help him in Viennese circles. During the 1880s he wrote most of the 300 songs which have ensured his fame, mostly in frantic bursts of creativity that were followed by fallow periods. These songs, usually settings of poems by Goethe, Morike and Eichendorf, have won him a reputation as Schubert's natural successor. In 1897 his mental health collapsed due to syphilis, and he had to enter a sanatorium, where he died.

Bibliography

P. Barford, *Mahler Symphonies and Songs,* University of Washington Press, Seattle, 1971

J. Chissell, *Brahms* (in the Great Composer series), Faber and Faber, London, 1977

E. Gartenberg, *Mahler: The Man and His Music,* Schirmer Books, New York, 1978

K. Geiringer, *Brahms: His Life and Works,* Da Capo, New York, 1981

H. de la Grange, *Mahler,* Doubleday, New York, 1974

D. Greene, *Mahler: Consciousness and Temporality,* Gordon and Breach, New York, 1984

J. Harrison, *Brahms and his Four Symphonies,* Da Capo, New York, 1971

P. Holmes, *Brahms: His Life and Times,* Hippocrene Books, New York, 1984

I. Keys, *Brahms Chamber Music,* University of Washington Press, Seattle, 1973

N. del Mar, *Mahler's Sixth Symphony: A Study,* Da Capo, New York, 1982

K. Martner (ed), *Gustav Mahler: Selected Letters 1877-1911,* Faber and Faber, London, 1979

D. Matthews, *Brahms Piano Music,* University of Washington Press, Seattle, 1978

D. Mitchell, *Gustav Mahler: The Early Years,* Faber and Faber, London, 1974

D. Mitchell, *Gustav Mahler: The Wunderhorn Years,* Faber and Faber, London, 1975

D. Mitchell, *Gustav Mahler: Songs and Symphonies of Life and Death,* Faber and Faber, London, 1985

B. Walter, *Gustav Mahler,* Da Capo, New York, 1970

Index

Note Page numbers in italic refer to illustrations.